LI-USA, Women's Auxiliary
Ahmadiyya Muslim Community
716-689-4820
womeninislam@lajnausa.net
www.alislam.org

W9-CBO-299

WORLD CRISIS
AND
THE PATHWAY TO PEACE

WORLD CRISIS

AND

THE PATHWAY TO PEACE

A Compilation of Speeches and Letters

of

Mirza Masroor Ahmad

Imam and the Head of the Worldwide Aḥmadiyya Muslim Jamāʿat,
Fifth Successor to the Promised Messiah[as], may Allah the Almighty be his help

ISLAM INTERNATIONAL PUBLICATIONS LTD.

World Crisis and the Pathway to Peace

A Compilation of Speeches and Letters
of
Ḥaḍrat Mirza Masroor Ahmad
Imam and the Head of the Worldwide Aḥmadiyya Muslim Jamāʿat,
Fifth Successor to the Promised Messiah^{as}

First published in the UK 2012

© Islam International Publications Ltd.

Published by
Islam International Publications Ltd.
Islamabad, Sheephatch Lane
Tilford, Surrey GU10 2AQ, UK

Printed and bound in Great Britain by the MPG Books Group

For further information please visit:
www.alislam.org

ISBN 978-1-84880-079-3

CONTENTS

Ḥaḍrat Mirza Masroor Ahmad
Khalīfatul Masīḥ V

ABOUT THE AUTHOR

His Holiness, Mirza Masroor Ahmad, Khalīfatul-Masīḥ V[aba], is the supreme head of the worldwide Aḥmadiyya Muslim Community. He is the fifth successor and great grandson of the Promised Messiah and Reformer, Ḥaḍrat Mirza Ghulam Ahmad[as] of Qadian.

His Holiness was born on September 15, 1950 in Rabwah, Pakistan to the late Mirza Mansoor Ahmad and the late Nāṣirah Begum Ahmad. Upon completing his Masters Degree in Agricultural Economics in 1977 from the Agriculture University in Faisalabad, Pakistan, he formally dedicated his life to the service of Islam. His altruistic endeavours took him to Ghana in 1977 where, for several years, he served as a principal of various Aḥmadiyya Muslim schools. He helped to inaugurate the Aḥmadiyya Secondary School Salaga, where he served as principal for the school's first two years.

Elected to the lifelong position of Khalīfah (Caliph) of the Aḥmadiyya Muslim Community on 22nd April 2003, he serves as the worldwide spiritual and administrative head of an international religious organization with tens of millions of members spread across 200 countries.

Since being elected Khalīfah, His Holiness has led a worldwide campaign to convey the peaceful message of Islam, through all forms of print and digital media. Under his leadership, national branches of the Ahmadiyya Muslim Community have launched campaigns that reflect the true and peaceful teachings of Islam. Ahmadi Muslims the world over are engaged in grassroots efforts to distribute millions of 'Peace' leaflets to Muslims and non-Muslims alike, host interfaith and peace symposia and present exhibitions of The Holy Qur'an to present its true and noble message. These campaigns have received worldwide media coverage and demonstrate that Islam champions peace, loyalty to one's country of residence and service to humanity.

In 2004, His Holiness launched the annual National Peace Symposium in which guests from all walks of life come together to exchange ideas on the promotion of peace and harmony. Each year, the symposium attracts many serving ministers, parliamentarians, politicians, religious leaders and other dignitaries.

His Holiness has travelled globally to promote and facilitate service to humanity. Under the leadership of His Holiness, the Ahmadiyya Muslim Community has built a number of schools and hospitals that provide high class facilities in remote parts of the world.

His Holiness, Mirza Masroor Ahmad[aba] currently resides in London, England. As spiritual leader of Ahmadi Muslims all over the world, he vigorously champions the cause of Islam through a refreshing message of peace and compassion.

PUBLISHERS' NOTE

Please note that, in the translation that follows, words given in parentheses ( ) are the words of the Promised Messiah[as]. If any explanatory words or phrases are added by the translator for the purpose of clarification, they are put in square brackets [ ]. Footnotes given by the publishers are marked '[Publishers]'. All references, unless otherwise specified, are from the English translation of the Holy Quran by Ḥaḍrat Maulavī Sher Ali[ra].

The following abbreviations have been used. Readers are urged to recite the full salutations when reading the book:

sa   *ṣallallāhu 'alaihi wa sallam*, meaning 'may peace and blessings of Allah be upon him,' is written after the name of the Holy Prophet Muhammad[sa].

as   *'alaihis-salām*, meaning 'may peace be on him,' is written after the name of Prophets other than the Holy Prophet Muhammad[sa].

ra   *raḍiyallāhu 'anhu/'anhā/'anhum*, meaning 'may Allah be pleased with him/her/them,' is written after the names of the Companions of the Holy Prophet Muhammad[sa] or of the Promised Messiah[as].

aba *ayyadahullāhu Taʿālā binaṣrihil-ʿAzīz*, meaning 'may Allah the Almighty help him with his powerful support,' is written after the name of the present Head of the Aḥmadiyya Muslim Jamāʿat, Ḥaḍrat Mirza Masroor Ahmad, Khalīfatul-Masīḥ V[aba].

In transliterating Arabic words we have adopted the following system established by the Royal Asiatic Society.

ا   at the beginning of a word, pronounced as *a, i, u* preceded by a very slight aspiration, like *h* in the English word *honour*.

ث   *th*, pronounced like *th* in the English word *thing*.

ح   *ḥ*, a guttural aspirate, stronger than *h*.

خ   *kh*, pronounced like the Scotch *ch* in *loch*.

ذ   *dh*, pronounced like the English *th* in *that*.

ص   *ṣ*, strongly articulated s.

ض   *ḍ*, similar to the English *th* in *this*.

ط   *ṭ*, strongly articulated palatal *t*.

ظ   *ẓ*, strongly articulated *z*.

ع   *ʿ*, a strong guttural, the pronunciation of which must be learnt by the ear

غ   *gh*, a sound approached very nearly in the *r grasseye* in French, and in the German *r*. It requires the muscles of the throat to be in the 'gargling' position whilst pronouncing it.

ق   *q*, a deep guttural *k* sound.

ء   *ʾ*, a sort of catch in the voice.

Short vowels are represented by:

    a   for ——— (like *u* in *bud*)

    i   for ——— (like *i* in *bid*)

    u for ——— (like *oo* in *wood*)

Long vowels by:

    ā for ——— or آ (like *a* in *father*);

    ī for ى ——— or ——— (like *ee* in *deep*);

    ū for و ——— (like *oo* in *root*);

Other:

    ai for ى ——— (like *i* in *site*);

    au for و ——— (resembling *ou* in *sound*)

The consonants not included in the above list have the same phonetic value as in the principal languages of Europe. While the Arabic ن is represented by *n*, we have indicated the Urdu ں as *ṅ*. Curved commas are used in the system of transliteration, ' for ع, ' for ء.

We have not transliterated Arabic words which have become part of English language, e.g. Islam, Quran, Hadith, Mahdi, jihad, Ramadan and ummah. The Royal Asiatic Society rules of transliteration for names of persons, places and other terms, could not be followed throughout the book as many of the names contain non-Arabic characters and carry a local transliteration and pronunciation style which in itself is also not consistent either.

The Publishers

FOREWORD

The purpose of Islam is to teach man the ways of attaining peace, both with himself and with his Creator. Under Divine direction, over 1,400 years ago, Ḥaḍrat Muhammad[sa], the Holy Founder of Islam, began the process of delivering this message to humanity. He made every effort to ensure that this message was conveyed as widely as possible and he took the extraordinary step of personally writing to the greatest kings and leaders of his time assuring them that if they would adopt the teachings of Islam they would be blessed with peace and prosperity.

Today, in this age and time, and in fulfilment of the prophecies of the Holy Prophet Muhammad[sa], God raised Ḥaḍrat Mirza Ghulam Ahmad[as], a true and most sincere servant of the Holy Prophet[sa], to rejuvenate the faith and instil the love of God in the hearts of men so that they may again learn the ways of peace and avoid destruction.

The letters sent recently to the leaders of the world by His Holiness, Mirza Masroor Ahmad (may Allah be his help), Fifth Successor to the Promised Messiah[as], are a continuation of the same work begun by the Holy Prophet[sa] fourteen centuries earlier.

His Holiness has also travelled widely to address in person the people in charge of running the world's greatest nations. His speeches and letters warn of a spiralling world crisis that is the natural outcome of unjust and inhumane financial and political policies that ceaselessly escalate tensions between peoples of the world.

The solution to the world's current dilemma, His Holiness says, lies in following the Quranic teachings of absolute justice. He urges the world leaders to pursue policies that are based on equality, justice, and religious freedom, and stop pursuing policies that are designed with short-sighted temporary self-gains in mind and rely on unjust and unfair exploitation of weaker nations and their natural resources.

May God, of His Grace and Mercy, open the hearts of the people to the acceptance of this message. (*Āmīn*).

The preparation of this book was entrusted to Usman Nasir Choudhary, based in USA. He was assisted by Salman Sajid, Abdul-Wahab Mirza, Dr. Waseem Sayed and Maryam Choudhary. I also appreciate the assistance of Amer Safir, Chief Editor and Manager of The Review of Religions, and Omair Aleem, In-charge Makhzan-e-Tasaweer. May Allah the Almighty reward all of them abundantly, (*Āmīn*).

Munir-ud-Din Shams
Additional Wakīlut-Taṣnīf,
London
August 2012

INTRODUCTION

The world is passing through very turbulent times. The global economic crisis continues to manifest newer and graver dangers almost every week. The similarities to the period just before the Second World War continue to be cited and it seems clear that events are moving the world at an unprecedented pace towards a horrific third world war. There is an overwhelming sense that things are quickly getting out of control and the people are looking for someone to step on to the stage to offer concrete, solid, guidance in which they can have confidence and that speaks to their heart and mind alike and gives them hope that there is a path that can lead to peace. The consequences of a nuclear war are so catastrophic that none dare even think about them.

Here, in this book, we have gathered the guidance put forth by Ḥaḍrat Mirza Masroor Ahmad, the Head of the worldwide Ahmadiyya Muslim Community. Over the past several years, as events have unfolded, he has been fearless in announcing to the world where things are heading—not to create alarm but to prepare them to think about how the world has arrived in this state of being and how it can avert disaster and chart a course to peace and security for all the people that inhabit this global village. He has forthrightly proclaimed that the only way to insure peace is for the world to adopt the ways of humility and justice and to humbly, submissively, turn to God; for man to become humane; for the strong to treat the weak with dignity and respect and justice and for the weak and poor to also to show gratitude and adopt the ways of truth and righteousness and for all to turn to their Creator in utter humility and total sincerity.

Again and again he has reminded one and all that the way back from the brink of disaster is for nations to make justice an absolute requirement of their dealings with each other. Even if there is enmity between them they need to still observe justice because history has taught us that this is the only way to eliminate all traces of future hatreds and thus build a lasting peace.

This is the teaching of the Holy Quran that he has emphasized in his letters to the leaders of the world:

> **And let not the enmity of a people, that they hindered you from the Sacred Mosque, incite you to transgress. And help one another in righteousness and piety; but help not one another in sin and transgression. And fear Allah; surely, Allah is severe in punishment.** (ch. 5: v. 3)

In his letter to the Prime Minister of Israel, he wrote:

> Hence, it is my request to you that instead of leading the world into the grip of a World War, make maximum efforts to save the world from a global catastrophe. Instead of resolving disputes with force, you should try to resolve

them through dialogue, so that we can gift our future generations with a bright future rather than 'gift' them with disability and defects.

To the President of the Islamic Republic of Iran, he admonished:

There is currently great agitation and restlessness in the world. In some areas small-scale wars have broken out, while in other places the superpowers act on the pretext of trying to bring about peace. Each country is engaged in activities to either help or oppose other countries, but the requirements of justice are not being fulfilled. It is with regret that if we now observe the current circumstances of the world, we find that the foundation for another world war has already been laid.

To President Obama, he stated:

As we are all aware, the main causes that led to the Second World War were the failure of League of Nations and the economic crisis, which began in 1932. Today, leading economists state that there are numerous parallels between the current economic crisis and that of 1932. We observe that political and economic problems have once again led to wars between smaller nations, and to internal discord and discontentment becoming rife within these countries. This will ultimately result in certain powers emerging to the helm of government, who will lead us to a world war. If in the smaller countries conflicts cannot be resolved through politics or diplomacy, it will lead to new blocs and groupings to form in the world. This will be the precursor for the outbreak of a Third World War. Hence, I believe that now, rather than focusing on the *progress* of the world, it is more important and indeed essential, that we urgently increase our efforts to save the world from this destruction. There is an urgent need for mankind to recognise its One God, Who is our Creator, as this is the only guarantor for the survival of humanity; otherwise, the world will continue to rapidly head towards self-destruction.

To Premier Wen Jiabao of the State of the People's Republic of China, he wrote:

It is my prayer that the leaders of the world act with wisdom and do not allow mutual enmities between nations and people on a small-scale to erupt into a global conflict.

And to the Prime Minister of the United Kingdom, he wrote:

It is my request that at every level and in every direction we must try our level best to extinguish the flames of hatred. Only if we are successful in this effort, will we be enabled to guarantee brighter futures for our generations to come. However, if we fail in this task, there should be no doubt in our minds that as result of nuclear warfare, our future generations everywhere will have to bear the horrific consequences of our actions and they will never forgive their elders for leading the world into a global catastrophe. I again remind you that Britain is also one of those countries that can and does exert influence in the developed world as well as in developing countries. You can guide this world, if you so desire, by fulfilling the requirements of equity and justice. Thus, Britain and other major powers should play their role towards establishing world peace. May God the Almighty enable you and other world leaders to understand this message.

It is our sincere prayer that the guidance collected herein may prove a source of guidance for mankind in this time of great danger so that by acting on the principles of justice and humility and by turning to God, man may be blessed with a lasting peace! (*Āmīn*).

The Publishers

SPEECHES

ISLAMIC PERSPECTIVE
ON THE GLOBAL CRISIS

THE BRITISH PARLIAMENT, THE HOUSE OF COMMONS
LONDON, UK, 2008

Preface

Historic Address by Ḥaḍrat Mirza Masroor Ahmad[aba], Khalīfatul-Masīḥ V, Head of the worldwide Ahmadiyya Muslim Community at the House of Commons (British Parliament) on 22 October 2008.

The reception was organised by Justine Greening, MP for Putney, home to the Fazl Mosque, the Headquarters of the Ahmadiyya Muslim Community, in honour of the completion of 100 years of *Khilāfat-e-Aḥmadiyya*.

In attendance at the reception were Gillian Merron MP, Rt Hon Hazel Blears MP, Alan Keen MP, Dominic Grieve MP, Simon Hughes MP, Lord Eric Avebury and also distinguished members of the press, politicians and professionals.

Islamic Perspective on the Global Crisis

Bismillāhir-Raḥmānir-Raḥīm—In the Name of Allah, the Gracious, Ever Merciful.

First of all I would like to thank all of the respected and honourable guests, MPs and Right Honourables who have allowed a leader of a religious organisation to say a few words to you. I am most grateful to our respected MP, Justine Greening, Member of Parliament of our area, who has done so much in organising this event for the sake of a small community of her constituency on the occasion of its Khilāfat Centenary. That shows her greatness, open heartedness and the concern about the sentiments of every people and community living in her constituency.

Although the Ahmadiyya Muslim Community is a small community, it is a standard-bearer and the representative of the true teachings of Islam. Nevertheless, I must say that every Ahmadi who lives in Great Britain is an extremely loyal citizen of the country and loves it; and this is because of the teachings of our Prophet[sa] who instructed us that the love of one's country is an integral part of one's faith.* The teaching of Islam has been further elaborated and emphasised by the Founder of the Ahmadiyya Community, whom we believe to be the Promised Messiah[as] and the Reformer of this Age.

He said that by announcing his claim God Almighty has placed two burdens upon him. One is the right of God and the other is right of God's creation. He went on to say that discharging the rights owed to God's creation was the most difficult and delicate challenge.**

With reference to Khilāfat, you may fear that a time might come when history repeats itself and wars may start as a result of this form of leadership. Let me assure you, however, that although this accusation is laid against Islam, God Willing, the Ahmadiyya Khilāfat will always be known as the standard-bearer of peace and harmony in the world, as well as be loyal to the country in which members reside. The Ahmadiyya Khilāfat is also here to perpetuate and continue the mission of the Messiah and Mahdi, and so there is absolutely no reason to fear the Khilāfat. This Khilāfat draws the attention of members of the Community towards fulfilling these two obligations for which the Promised Messiah[as] came, and as a result, tries to create peace and harmony in the world.

Now, because of the time constraint, I come to the subject matter. If we survey the last few centuries impartially, we will

---

* *Tafsīr-e-Ḥaqqī, Sūrah al-Qaṣaṣ*, no. 86, and *Fatḥul-Bārī fī Sharḥ Ṣaḥīḥ al-Bukhārī*, Bābo Qaulillāhi Ta'alā Wa'tul-boyūta… and *Tohfatul-Aḥwadhī Sharḥo Jāmi' it-Tirmadhī*, Bābo Mā Yaqūl

** *Malfūẓāt*, vol.1, p.326

notice that the wars over that period were not really religious wars. They were more geopolitical in nature. Even in today's conflicts and hostilities amongst nations, we notice that they arise from political, territorial and economic interests.

It is my fear that in view of the direction in which things are moving today, the political and economic dynamics of the countries of the world may lead to a world war. It is not only the poorer countries of the world, but also the richer nations that are being affected by this. Therefore, it is the duty of the superpowers to sit down and find a solution to save humanity from the brink of disaster.

Britain is also one of those countries that can and does exert influence in the developed world as well as in developing countries. You can guide the world, if you so desire, by fulfilling the requirement of equity and justice.

If we look at the recent past, Britain ruled over many countries and left behind a high standard of justice and religious freedom, especially in the sub-continent of India and Pakistan. The Ahmadiyya Muslim Community has witnessed this, and the Founder[as] of the Ahmadiyya Community has greatly praised the British Government on its policies of justice and granting of religious freedom. When the Founder[as] of the Ahmadiyya Community congratulated Her Majesty Queen Victoria on her Diamond Jubilee, and conveyed to her the message of Islam, he specially prayed that, in view of the manner in which the British Government discharges the requirements of justice with equity, may God Almighty reward it generously.

So, our history shows that we have always acknowledged this justice whenever displayed by Britain, and we hope that in future too, justice will remain a defining characteristic of the British Government, not only in religious matters, but in all respects, and that you never forget your good qualities of the past.

Today, there is great agitation and restlessness in the world. We are seeing small-scale wars erupting, while in some places, the superpowers are claiming to try and bring about peace. If the requirements of justice are not fulfilled, the conflagration and flames of these local wars can escalate and embroil the whole world. Therefore, it is my humble request to you to save the world from destruction!

Now, I will briefly mention what the teachings of Islam are to bring about peace in the world, or how peace can be established in the world in the light of these teachings. It is my prayer that to create peace in the world those who are being addressed initially, that is to say the Muslims, may be able to act upon them, but it is a duty of all the countries of the world, all the superpowers or governments, to act upon.

In this day and age when the world has literally shrunk to a global village in a way that could not have been imagined previously, we must realise our responsibilities as human beings and should try to pay attention to solving those issues of human rights that can help to establish peace in the world. Clearly, this attempt must be based on fair play and on fulfilling all the requirements of justice.

Amongst the problems of today, one problem has arisen, if not directly, then indirectly, because of religion. Some groups of Muslims use unlawful means and suicide bombers, bombing in the name of religion to kill and harm non-Muslims including soldiers and innocent civilians, and at the same time to brutally kill innocent Muslims and children. This cruel act is totally unacceptable in Islam.

Due to this ghastly behaviour of some Muslims, a totally wrong impression has developed in non-Muslim countries, and as a result, some parts of the society talk openly against Islam, whilst the others, even though do not speak openly, do not carry a good opinion about Islam in their hearts. This has created distrust in the hearts of the people of Western and non-Muslim countries about Muslims, and because of this attitude of a few Muslims, instead of the situation improving, the reaction of non-Muslims is getting worse by the day.

A primary example of this erroneous reaction is the attack on the character of the Holy Prophet[sa] of Islam and on the Holy Quran, the Sacred Book of the Muslims. In this regard, the attitude of British politicians, whatever their party, and of intellectuals in Britain, has been different to that shown by the politicians of some other countries, and I thank you for that. What can the benefit be of hurting such sensitivities apart from increasing hatred and dislike? This hatred spurs certain extremist Muslims into committing 'un-Islamic' deeds, which in turn, provides further opportunity to a number of non-Muslims to air their opposition.

However, those who are not extremists and who deeply love the Holy Prophet[sa] of Islam, are terribly hurt by these attacks and, in this, the Ahmadiyya Jamāʻat (Community) is at the forefront. Our single most important task is to show the world the perfect character of the Holy Prophet[sa] and the beautiful teachings of Islam. We, who respect and revere all the Prophets (peace be upon them all) and believe all of them to be the Messengers sent by God, cannot say anything disrespectful against any of them;

but we are very saddened when we hear baseless, untrue allegations against our Prophet[sa].

Nowadays, when the world again is getting divided into blocs; extremism is escalating; and the financial and economic situation is worsening, there is an urgent need to end all kinds of hatred and to lay the foundations of peace. This can only be done by respecting all kinds of sentiments of each other. If this is not done properly, honestly and with virtue, it will escalate into uncontrollable circumstances. I appreciate that economically sound Western countries have generously permitted the people of poor or underdeveloped nations to settle in their respective countries, among whom are Muslims as well.

True justice requires that the sentiments and the religious practices of these people should also be honoured. This is the way by which the peace of mind of people can be kept in tact. We should remember that when the peace of mind of a person is disturbed then the peace of mind of the society is also affected.

As I said earlier, I am grateful to the British legislators and politicians for fulfilling the requirements of justice and for not interfering in this way. This, in fact, is the teaching of Islam that is given to us by the Holy Quran. The Holy Quran declares that:

There should be no compulsion in religion... (ch. 2: v. 257)

This commandment not only counters the accusation that Islam was spread by the sword, but also tells Muslims that acceptance of faith is a matter between man and his God, and you should not interfere in this in any way. Everyone is permitted to live according to his faith and to perform his religious rituals. However, if there are any practices performed in the name of religion that harm others and go against the law of the land, then the law enforcers of that State can come into action, because if there is any cruel ritual being practised in any religion, it cannot be the teaching of any Prophet of God.

This is the fundamental principle for establishing peace at the local level as well as the international level.

Moreover, Islam teaches us that if as a result of your change of faith, any society, or group or a government tries to interfere in the observance of your religious practice, and thereafter the circumstances change in your favour, then always remember that you must carry no malice or ill-will. You should not think of taking revenge but should rather establish justice and equity. The Holy Quran says:

> O ye who believe! Be steadfast in the cause of Allah, bearing witness in equity; and let not a people's enmity incite you to act otherwise than with justice. Be *always* just, that is nearer to righteousness. And fear Allah. Surely Allah is aware of what you do. (ch. 5: v. 9)

This is the teaching for peace in society. Never depart from justice even for your enemy. The early history of Islam shows us that this teaching was followed and all the demands of justice were fulfilled. I cannot give too many examples of this but history bears testimony to the fact that after the Victory of Makkah, the Holy Prophet[sa] did not take any revenge from those who had tormented him but forgave them and allowed them to adhere to their respective faiths. Today, peace can be established only if all requirements of justice are met for the enemy, not only in wars against religious extremists, but also in all other wars. And only such peace is long-lasting.

In the last century, two world wars were fought. Whatever the causes were, if we look deeply, only one cause stands out; and it is that justice was not properly administered in the first instance. As a reaction, what was considered to be an extinguished fire turned out to be cinders that kept on burning slowly, eventually bursting into flames and enveloping the whole world a second time.

Today, restlessness is increasing and wars and actions to maintain peace are becoming the forerunners for another world war. Moreover, the present economic and social problems will be the source of aggravating the situation.

The Holy Quran has given some golden principles for establishing peace in the world. It is an established fact that greed causes enmity to grow. Sometimes it manifests itself in territorial expansion or the seizing of the natural resources or, indeed, in impressing the superiority of some upon others. This leads to cruelty, whether it is at the hands of merciless despots who usurp the rights of people and prove their supremacy in pursuit of their vested interests, or it is at the hands of an invading force. Sometimes, the cries and anguish of the cruelly treated people call out to the outside world.

But be that as it may, we have been taught the following golden principle by the Holy Prophet of Islam[sa], which is: help both the afflicted and the cruel.

The Companions of the Prophet[sa] enquired that whereas they could understand helping the afflicted, how could they help a cruel person? The Prophet[sa] responded by saying, 'By stopping his hand from committing cruelty because his excess in cruelty will make him worthy of God's punishment.'* So, out of mercy, you try to save him. This principle extends beyond the smallest fibres of society to the international level. In this connection, the Holy Quran says:

And if two parties of believers fight *against each other*, make peace between them; then *if after that* one of them transgresses against the other, fight the party that transgresses until it returns to the command of Allah. Then if it returns, make peace between them with equity, and act justly. Verily, Allah loves the just. (ch. 49: v. 10)

Though this teaching is about Muslims, yet by adhering to this principle, the foundation of peace on a worldwide basis can be laid.

In order to maintain peace, it has been explained at the outset that the foremost requirement is justice. And, despite abiding by the principle of justice, if efforts to make peace are unsuccessful, then unite and fight collectively against the party that has transgressed and continue until such a time that the transgressing party is ready to make peace. Once the transgressing party is ready to make peace, the requirement of justice is: do not seek revenge, do not impose restrictions or embargoes. By all means, keep an

---

* *Ṣaḥīḥ al-Bukhārī, Kitābul-Ikrāh*, Bābo Yamīnir-Rajuli Li Ṣāḥibihi... Hadith no. 6952...

eye on the transgressor but at the same time try and improve his situation.

In order to end the unrest prevalent in some countries of the world today—and unfortunately, some Muslim countries are prominent amongst them—it should be analysed in particular by those nations that have the power to veto, to determine whether or not justice has been properly dispensed. Whenever help is needed, the hands are stretched towards the powerful nations.

As I stated before, we bear testimony to the fact that the history of the British government has always upheld justice and this has encouraged me to draw your attention to some of these matters.

Another principle that we have been taught for restoring peace in the world is not to covetously eye the wealth of others. The Holy Quran says:

> **And strain not thy eyes after what We have bestowed on some classes of them to enjoy *for a short time*—the splendour of the present world—that We may try them thereby...** (ch. 20: v. 132)

Greed for any envy of the wealth of others is a cause of increasing restlessness in the world. On a personal basis, keeping up with the Joneses, as the saying goes, has resulted in unending greed and destroyed social peace. Greedy competition on a national basis started and led to the destruction of world peace. This is proven by history and every sensible person can assess that the desire for the wealth of others causes envy and greed to grow and is the source of loss.

This is why God Almighty says that one should keep an eye on one's own resources and derive benefit from them. The effort to make territorial gains is for seeking the benefit of that territory's natural resources. The grouping of nations and the making of power blocs are to procure the natural resources of some countries. In this regard, a number of authors who had previously worked as advisors to the governments have written books detailing how some of the countries endeavour to get control of the resources of other nations. How far the writers are truthful is best known to them, and God knows best, but the situation that emerges from reading these accounts causes serious anguish in the hearts of those who are loyal to their poor countries, and is a major reason for the growth in terrorism and the race for weapons of mass destruction.

Nowadays, the world considers itself more sober, conscious and educated than in the past. Even in the poor countries there are such intelligent souls who have greatly excelled in education in their respective fields. Highly intellectual minds work together in large research centres of the world. Under such circumstances, one should have imagined that people would have joined together and jointly tried to end the wrong ways of thinking and the follies of the past that had resulted in animosities and had led to horrific wars. The God-given intellect and scientific progress should have been used for the betterment of humanity and for devising permissible methods of deriving benefits from one another's resources.

God has bestowed each and every country with natural resources that should have been fully utilised to turn the world into a haven of peace. God has gifted many countries with an excellent climate and environment for growing different crops. Had proper planning been adopted to use modern technology for agriculture, the economy would have strengthened and hunger could have been eliminated from the earth.

Those countries that have been endowed with mineral resources should be allowed to develop and trade at fair prices and openly, and one country should benefit from the resources of the other country. So, this would be the right way, the way that is preferred by God Almighty.

God Almighty sends His messengers to the people so that they can show them the ways that bring people closer to God. At the same time, God says that there is complete freedom in matters of faith. According to our beliefs, reward and punishment will be after death as well. But under the system that God has set up, when the cruelty is inflicted on His creation and justice and fair play are ignored, then by the laws of nature, the after-effects can be seen in this world as well. Severe reactions to such injustice are observed and there can be no guarantee about the reaction being right or wrong.

The true way to conquer the world is that every effort should be made to give the poorer nations their due status.

A major issue today is the economic crisis of what has been termed as the credit crunch. Strange as it may sound, the evidence points towards one fact. The Holy Quran guides us by saying: avoid interest because interest is such a curse that it is a danger for domestic, national and international peace. We have been warned that he who accepts interest will one day be as one whom Satan has smitten with insanity. So, we Muslims have been warned that in order to avoid such a situation, stop dealing in interest because money that you get for interest does not enhance your wealth, although on the face of it, it may seem to you that it is increasing. Inevitably, a time comes when its true effects emerge. Furthermore, we have been cautioned that we are not allowed to enter into the business of interest, with the warning that if you do so, it will be a war against God.

This factor is obvious from today's credit crunch. In the beginning there were individuals who borrowed money to buy property; but before they could see ownership of the property they used to die burdened with the debt. But now there are governments that are burdened with debt and smitten as if with insanity. Large companies have become bankrupt. Some banks and financial institution have folded or been bailed out and this situation prevails in every country, regardless of its being rich or poor. You know better than I do about this crisis. The money of the depositors has been wiped off. Now it depends upon governments as to how and to what extent to protect them. But for the time being, the peace of mind of the families, business-men and leaders of the governments in most countries of the world has all but been destroyed.

Does this situation not compel us to think that the world is heading to the logical conclusion whose warning was given to us well in advance? God knows better what the further consequences of this situation will be.

God Almighty has said: Come towards peace that can only be guaranteed when there is pure and wholesome trade and when resources are put into usage in a proper and fair manner.

Now I end these brief points of our teachings with a reminder that the true peace of the world lies only in turning towards God. May God enable the world to understand this point; only then will they be able to discharge the rights of others.

Finally, I am grateful to all of you again for coming here and listening to me.

Thank you very much.

ISLAM'S TEACHINGS OF LOYALTY AND LOVE FOR ONE'S NATION

MILITARY HEADQUARTERS
KOBLENZ, GERMANY, 2012

Islam's Teachings of Loyalty and Love for One's Nation

Bismillāhir-Raḥmānir-Raḥīm—In the Name of Allah, the Gracious, the Merciful.

Assalāmu ʿalaikum wa raḥmatullāhe wa barakātohū—peace and blessings of Allah be upon you all.

I would like to first of all take this opportunity to thank all of you for inviting me to your headquarters and giving me the opportunity to say a few words. As the Head of the Ahmadiyya Muslim Community, I would like to speak to you about the teachings of Islam. However, this is such a vast topic, that to cover it in just one function or in a short time is impossible. Thus, it is necessary that I limit myself to one aspect of Islam to focus on and speak to you about.

Whilst contemplating which facet of Islam I should address, I received a request from the National President of our Community here in Germany, Abdullah Wagishauser, in which he asked me to speak about Islam's teachings in relation to love and loyalty to one's nation. This helped me make my decision. Thus, I shall now speak to you briefly about certain aspects of Islam's teachings in this regard.

It is very easy to simply speak of, or hear the words, 'loyalty and love for one's nation.' However, in reality these few words encompass meanings that are wide-ranging, beautiful and of tremendous depth. Indeed, to fully comprehend and understand what these words truly mean and what they require is actually very difficult. In any case, in the short time available, I will try to explain Islam's concept of loyalty and love for one's nation.

First and foremost, a fundamental principle of Islam is that a person's words and deeds should never manifest any form of double standards or hypocrisy. True loyalty requires a relationship built on sincerity and integrity. It requires what a person displays on the surface to be the same as what lies beneath. In terms of nationality, these principles are of the utmost importance. Therefore, it is essential for a citizen of any country to establish a relationship of genuine loyalty and faithfulness to his nation. It does not matter whether he is a born citizen, or whether he gains citizenship later in life, either through immigration or by any other means.

Loyalty is a great quality, and the people who have displayed this attribute to the highest degree and best standards, are the Prophets of God. Their love and bond with God was so strong that in all matters they kept in view His commands and strived to fully implement them, no matter what. This illustrated their commitment to Him and their perfect standards of loyalty. Hence, it is their standards of loyalty that we should use as an example and model. However, before proceeding any further, it is necessary to understand what is actually meant by 'loyalty'.

According to the teachings of Islam, the definition and true meaning of 'loyalty' is the unequivocal fulfilment of one's pledges and covenants at every level and under all circumstances, regardless of difficulty. This is the true standard of faithfulness required by Islam. At various places in the Holy Quran, Allah has instructed Muslims that they must fulfil their pledges and covenants, because they will be held to account by Him over all undertakings that they have made. The Muslims have been instructed to fulfil all covenants, including those made with God Almighty, and also all other pledges they have made, according to their respective degrees of importance.

In this context, a question that could arise in the minds of people is that because Muslims claim that God and His religion are of paramount importance to them, thus it follows that their pledge of loyalty to God will be their first priority, and that their covenant to God will be what they value above all else and which they endeavour to fulfil. Therefore, the belief may arise that a Muslim's loyalty to his nation and his pledge to uphold the laws of the land will only be of secondary importance to him. Thus, he may be willing to sacrifice his pledge to his country on certain occasions.

To answer this question, I would firstly like to inform you that the Holy Prophet Muhammad (peace be upon him) himself taught that the 'love for one's nation is a part of faith.' Thus, sincere patriotism is a requirement in Islam. To truly love God and Islam requires a person to love his nation. It is quite clear, therefore, that there can be no conflict of interest between a person's love for

God, and love for his country. As love for one's country has been made a part of Islam, it is quite clear that a Muslim must strive to reach the highest standards of loyalty to his chosen country, because that is a means of reaching God and becoming close to Him. Hence, it is impossible that the love a true Muslim holds for God could ever prove to be an impediment or barrier preventing him from displaying true love and faithfulness towards his country. Unfortunately, we find that in certain countries, religious rights are curtailed or even completely denied. Therefore, another question that can arise is whether those people who are persecuted by their state can still maintain a relationship of love and loyalty to their nation and country. With great sadness, I should inform you that these circumstances exist in Pakistan, where the Government has actually legislated against our Community. These anti-Ahmadiyya laws are practically enforced. Thus in Pakistan, all Ahmadi Muslims have been officially declared by law to be 'non-Muslims'. They are, therefore, forbidden from calling themselves 'Muslim'. The Ahmadis in Pakistan are also prohibited from worshipping in the way Muslims do, or acting in accordance with any Islamic practice or custom that could identify them as a Muslim. Thus, the state itself in Pakistan has deprived members of our Community from their basic human right to worship.

Bearing in mind this state of affairs, it is quite natural to wonder how, in such circumstances, can Ahmadi Muslims follow the laws of the land? How can they continue to display loyalty to the nation? Here I should clarify that where such extreme circumstances exist, then the law, and loyalty to the nation, become two separate issues. We, Ahmadi Muslims, believe that religion is a personal matter for every individual to determine for himself and that there should be no compulsion in matters of faith. Thus, where the law comes to interfere with this right, undoubtedly, it is an act of great cruelty and persecution. Indeed, such state-sanctioned persecution, which has occurred throughout the ages, has been condemned by the vast majority.

If we glance at the history of Europe, we find that people in this Continent have also been the victims of religious persecution, and as a result, many thousands of people had to migrate from one country to the next. All fair-minded historians, governments and people have deemed this to be persecution, and extremely cruel. In such circumstances, Islam advocates that where persecution goes beyond all limits and becomes unbearable, then at that time, a person should leave the town or country and migrate to a place where he is free to practise his religion in peace. However, alongside this guidance, Islam also teaches that under no circumstances should any individual take the law into his own hands and nor should he partake in any schemes or conspiracies against his country. This is an absolutely clear and unequivocal command given by Islam.

Despite the grave persecution they face, millions of Ahmadis continue to live in Pakistan. Despite being subjected to such sustained discrimination and cruelty in all aspects of their lives, they continue to keep a relationship of total loyalty and a true allegiance to the country. Whichever field they work in or wherever they are based, they are constantly engaged in trying to help the nation to progress and succeed. For decades, the opponents of Ahmadiyyat have tried to allege that Ahmadis are not loyal to Pakistan, but they have never been able to prove this or show any evidence to support their claims; instead, the truth is that whenever there has been a need to make any sacrifice for the sake of Pakistan, for the sake of their country, Ahmadi Muslims have always stood at the forefront and been constantly ready to make every sacrifice for the sake of the country.

Despite themselves being a victim and target of the law, it is Ahmadi Muslims who follow and abide by the laws of the land better than anyone else. This is because they are true Muslims, who follow true Islam. Another teaching given by the Holy Quran in relation to loyalty is that people should keep away from all things that are immodest, undesirable and that form any type of rebellion. A beautiful and distinguishing feature of Islam is that it does not just draw our attention to the final point of culmination, where the consequences are extremely dangerous; instead, it warns us about all of the smaller issues as well, which act as stepping stones leading mankind to a path paved with danger. Thus, if Islam's guidance is followed properly, then any issue can be resolved at the earliest point, before the situation gets out of hand.

For instance, an issue which can gravely harm a country is financial greed by individuals. Often, people get consumed by material desires that spiral beyond control, and such desires ultimately lead people to act in a disloyal fashion. Thus, such things can ultimately be a cause of treachery against one's country. Let me explain a bit. In Arabic the word *baghā* has been used to describe those people or those acts of people that cause harm to their countries. It refers to those who take part in wrong practices or who inflict harm on others. It also includes those people who commit fraud and so try to acquire things in an illegal or unjust manner. It refers to those people who transgress all limits and so cause harm and damage. Islam teaches that people who act in these ways cannot be expected to act in a loyal manner, because loyalty is intertwined with high moral values. Loyalty cannot exist without high moral values and high moral values cannot exist without loyalty. Whilst it is true that different people may have different views about high moral standards, yet the religion of Islam revolves solely around seeking God's pleasure. Thus, Muslims are instructed to always act in a manner that is pleasing to Him. In short, according to Islamic teachings, God Almighty has forbidden all forms off treachery or rebellion, whether against one's country or one's government. This is because rebellion or acting against the state is a threat to the peace and security of a nation. Indeed, where internal rebellion or opposition occurs, then it fans the flames of external opposition and encourages outsiders to take advantage of the internal disorder. Hence, the consequences of disloyalty to your nation can be far-reaching and extreme. Thus, anything that can cause harm to a nation is included in the term *baghā* that I have described. Keeping all of this in mind, loyalty to one's nation requires a person to display patience, to show morality and to follow the laws of the land.

Generally speaking, in the modern era, most governments are run democratically. Therefore if a person or group wishes to change the government, then they should do so by following the proper democratic process. They should make themselves heard by voting at the ballot box. Votes should not be cast on the basis of personal preferences or personal interests, but in fact, Islam teaches that a person's vote should be exercised with a sense of loyalty and love for his country. A person's vote should be cast with the betterment of the nation in mind. Therefore, a person should not look at his own priorities and from which candidate or party he can personally benefit; instead, a person should make his decision in a balanced way whereby he assesses which candidate or party will help the entire nation progress. The keys to government are a huge trust and thus they should only be handed over to the party who the voter honestly believes is best suited and most deserving. This is the true Islam, and this is true loyalty.

Indeed, in Chapter 4, verse 59 of the Holy Quran, Allah has commanded that a person should only hand over trusts to those who are entitled, and that when judging between people, he should make his decision with justice and honesty. Thus, loyalty to one's nation requires that the power of the government should be given to those who are truly entitled to it, so that the nation can progress and come to stand at the forefront amongst the nations of the world.

In many parts of the world we find that members of the public take part in strikes and protests against government policies. Furthermore, in certain Third World countries, the protesters vandalise or damage possessions and properties belonging either to the state or to private citizens. Though they may claim to be acting out of love, the truth is that such acts have nothing to do with loyalty or love for the nation. It should be remembered that even where protests or strikes are conducted peacefully, without recourse to criminal damage or violence, it still can have a very negative effect. This is because even peaceful protests often result in a loss of millions to the economy of the nation. Under no circumstances can such behaviour be considered to be an example of loyalty to the nation. A golden principle taught by the Founder of the Ahmadiyya Muslim Jamāʿat was that under all circumstances, we must always remain obedient to Allah, to the Prophets and to the rulers of our nation. This is the same teaching given in the Holy Quran. Hence, even where a country permits strikes or protests to take place, they should only be conducted to the extent where they do not harm or cause damage to the nation or to the economy.

Another question that often arises is whether Muslims can join the military forces of the Western countries, and if they are permitted to join, can they then partake in military attacks on Muslim countries? One underlying principle of Islam is that no person should assist in acts of cruelty. This key command must always remain at the forefront of any Muslim's mind. Where a Muslim country is attacked, because it has itself acted in a cruel and unjust manner and took the first step of aggression, then in such circumstances the Quran has instructed Muslim governments that they should stop the hand of the oppressor. This means they should stop the cruelty and endeavour to establish peace. Thus, in such circumstances to take action as a means to end cruelty is permissible. However, when the nation which transgresses reforms itself and adopts peace, then that country and its people should not be taken advantage of or be subjugated on the basis of false pretences or excuses. They should instead be granted normal state freedom and independence once again. The military ambition should thus be to establish peace, rather than to fulfil any vested interests.

In the same way, Islam permits all countries, whether Muslim or non-Muslim, the right to stop cruelty and oppression. Thus, if necessary, non-Muslim countries can attack Muslim countries to achieve these genuine aims. Muslims in those non-Muslim countries are allowed to join the armies of those non-Muslim countries and prevent the other country from cruelty. Where such circumstances truly exist then Muslim soldiers, whichever Western army they may be part of, must follow orders and fight if required in order to establish peace. If, however, a military makes a decision to attack another nation unjustly, and thus becomes the oppressor, then a Muslim has the option to leave the army, because then he would be assisting cruelty. By taking this decision it would not mean that he is being disloyal to his country. In fact, in such circumstances, loyalty to his country would demand that he should take such a step and counsel his own government that they should not allow themselves to fall to the same depths as those unjust governments and nations that act in a cruel way. If however, joining the army is compulsory and there is no way to leave, but his conscience is not clear, then the Muslim should leave the country, but cannot raise a voice against the law of the land. He should leave because a Muslim is not permitted to live in a country as a citizen, whilst at the same time, acting against the nation or siding with the opposition.

Thus these are just a few aspects of Islamic teachings, which guide all true Muslims towards the real requirements of loyalty and love for one's country. In the time available I have only been able to briefly touch upon this topic.

Thus in conclusion, I would like to say that today we observe that the world has become a global village. Mankind has become very closely knit together. The people of all nations, religions and cultures are found in all countries. This requires that the leaders of every nation should consider and respect the feelings and sentiments of all people. The leaders and their governments should strive to create laws that foster an environment and spirit of truth and justice, rather than making laws that are a means of causing distress and frustration to the people. Injustices and cruelties should be eliminated and instead we should strive for true justice. The best way to do this is that the world should come to recognise its Creator. Every form of loyalty should be linked to loyalty with God. If this occurs then we will come to witness with our own eyes that the very highest standards of loyalty will be established by the people of all countries and new avenues leading us to peace and security will open throughout the world.

Before ending, I would like to take this opportunity to thank all of you once again for inviting me today and for listening to what I have said. May God bless you all; and may God bless Germany.

Thank you very much.

THE DEVASTATING CONSEQUENCES
OF A NUCLEAR WAR AND THE
CRITICAL NEED FOR ABSOLUTE JUSTICE

9TH ANNUAL PEACE SYMPOSIUM
LONDON, UNITED KINGDOM, 2012

NATIONAL PEACE SYMPOSIUM
2012

Preface

On March 24, 2012, the 9th Annual Peace Symposium was held at the Baitul Futūḥ Mosque in Morden—the largest Mosque in Western Europe—organised by the Aḥmadiyya Muslim Jamāʿat (Community) in the UK. The event attracted an audience of more than 1000 people, including government ministers, ambassadors of state, members of both the House of Commons and the House of Lords, the Mayor of London, various other dignitaries, professionals, neighbours and guests from all walks of life. The theme of this year's Symposium was 'International Peace'. The 3rd Annual 'Aḥmadiyya Muslim Prize for the Advancement of Peace' was presented by Ḥaḍrat Mirza Masroor Ahmad[aba] to the charity, 'SOS Children's Villages UK,' in recognition of its continued efforts to alleviating the suffering of orphaned and abandoned children around the world and towards fulfilling its vision of 'a loving home for every child.'

Guests in attendance included:

- Rt Hon Justine Greening—MP, Secretary of State for Transport
- Jane Ellison—MP (Battersea)
- Seema Malhotra—MP (Feltham and Heston)
- Tom Brake—MP (Carlshalton and Wallington)
- Virendra Sharma—MP (Ealing and Southall)
- Lord Tariq Ahmad—of Wimbledon
- HE Wesley Momo Johnson—the Ambassador of Liberia
- HE Abdullah Al-Radhi—the Ambassador of Yemen
- HE Miguel Solano-Lopez—the Ambassador of Paraguay
- Commodore Martin Atherton—Naval Regional Commander
- Councillor Jane Cooper—the Worshipful Mayor of Wandsworth
- Councillor Milton McKenzie MBE—the Worshipful Mayor of Barking and Dagenham
- Councillor Amrit Mann—the Worshipful Mayor of Hounslow
- Siobhan Benita—independent Mayoral candidate for London
- Diplomats from several other countries including India, Canada, Indonesia and Guinea

The Devastating Consequences of a Nuclear War and the Critical Need for Absolute Justice

After reciting *tashahhud*, *ta'awwudh* and *bismillāh*, Ḥaḍrat Khalīfatul-Masīḥ V^[aba] said:

All our guests—*assalāmu 'alaikum wa raḥmatullāhe wa barakā-tohū*—peace and blessings of Allah be upon you all.

Today, after a period of one year, I once again have the opportunity to welcome all of our distinguished guests to this event. I am extremely grateful to all of you, as you have spared your time to come and attend today.

Indeed, most of you are well acquainted with this event which has come to be known as the 'Peace Symposium'. This event is organised each year by the Aḥmadiyya Muslim Community and is just one of our many efforts to try and fulfil our desire for peace to be established in the world.

In attendance today are some new friends, who are attending this function for the first time, whilst others are old friends who have supported our efforts for many years. Regardless, all of you are well-educated and share our desire for peace to be established in the world, and it is due to this desire that you are all attending this event.

All of you are here today with the heartfelt wish that the world comes to be filled with love, affection and friendship. It is this very attitude and these very values that the vast majority of the world longs for and which it stands in need of. In view of all of this, these are the reasons why all of you, who come from different backgrounds, nations and religions, are sitting in front of me today.

As I have said, we hold this conference each year and on each occasion, the same sentiment and hope is expressed by all of us, which is that peace in the world comes to be established before our very eyes; and so each year I also request all of you to endeavour to promote peace wherever you have the opportunity and with whoever you have contact. Furthermore, I also request all those who are linked to political parties or governments that they should also convey this message of peace within their circles of influence. It is essential that everyone is made aware that, for the establishment of world peace, there is a far greater need for high and principled moral values than ever before.

As far as the Aḥmadiyya Community is concerned, wherever and whenever the opportunity arises, we openly express and declare our view that there is only one way to save the world from the destruction and devastation that it is heading towards, and that is that we must all endeavour to spread love, affection and a sense of community. Most importantly, the world must come to recognize its Creator, Who is the One God. This is because it is the recognition of the Creator that leads us towards love and compassion for His Creation, and when this becomes part of our character, it is then that we become recipients of God's Love.

We constantly raise our voice calling for peace in the world, and it is the pain and anguish we feel in our hearts that inspires us to try and alleviate the suffering of mankind and to make the world we live in a better place. Indeed, this very function is just one of our many efforts towards achieving this goal.

As I have already said, all of you also hold these noble desires. Furthermore, I have repeatedly called on politicians and religious leaders to strive for peace. Yet, in spite of all of these efforts, we find that anxiety and turmoil continue to spread and increase throughout the world. In today's world we find so much strife, restlessness and disorder. In some countries members of the public are fighting and waging wars amongst themselves. In some nations the public is fighting against the government, or conversely the rulers are attacking their own people. Terrorist groups are fuelling anarchy and disorder to fulfil their vested interests and so they are arbitrarily killing innocent women, children and the elderly. In some countries, as a means to fulfil their own interests, political parties are warring with each other rather than coming together for the betterment of their nations. We also find some governments and countries are continuously casting their glances enviously in the direction of the resources of other nations. The major powers of the world are consumed by their efforts to maintain their supremacy, and leave no stone unturned in their efforts towards pursuing this goal.

Bearing all of this in mind, we find that neither the Aḥmadiyya

Community nor the majority of you, who are members of the public, have the power or authority to develop policies to bring positive change. This is because we do not hold any governmental power or office. In fact, I would go as far as to say that even the politicians, with whom we have developed friendly relations and who always agree with us when they are in our company, are also unable to speak out. Instead, their voices too are being drowned out and they are prevented from forwarding their views. This is either because they are forced to follow party policies, or perhaps due to external pressures from other world powers or political allies, which are weighing them down.

Nevertheless, we, who take part in this Peace Symposium each year, undoubtedly hold a desire for peace to be established and certainly we express our opinions and feelings that love, compassion and brotherhood should be established amongst all religions, all nationalities, all races and indeed, amongst all people. Unfortunately though, we are powerless to actually bring this vision to light. We do not have the authority or means to achieve the results that we long for.

I recall that a couple of years ago, in this very hall during our Peace Symposium, I delivered a speech detailing the ways and means for world peace to be established, and I also spoke about how the United Nations ought to function. Afterwards, our very dear and respected friend, Lord Eric Avebury, commented that the speech ought to have been delivered at the United Nations itself. Nevertheless, this was a display of his noble character that he was so generous and kind in his remarks. However, what I wish to say is that merely delivering or listening to a speech or lecture is not enough and will not lead to peace being established. In fact, the key requirement to fulfilling this primary goal is absolute justice and fairness in all matters. The Holy Quran, in Chapter 4, verse 136, has given us a golden principle and lesson, guiding us about this. It states that as a means to fulfil the requirements of justice, even if you have to bear witness and testify against yourself, your parents or your closest relatives and friends, then you must do so. This is true justice where personal interests are set aside for the common good.

If we think about this principle at a collective level, then we will realise that unfair lobbying techniques based on wealth and influence should be abandoned. Instead, the representatives and ambassadors of each nation should come forward with sincerity and with a desire to support the principles of fairness and equality. We must eliminate all forms of bias and discrimination, as this is the only means to bring about peace. If we look at the United Nations General Assembly or Security Council, we find that often statements or speeches made there receive great praise and acknowledgement, but such tributes are meaningless because the real decisions have already been predetermined.

Thus, where decisions are made on the basis of the pressure or the lobbying of the major powers, as opposed to just and truly democratic means, then such speeches are rendered hollow, meaningless and serve only as pretence to deceive the outside world. Nevertheless, all of this does not mean that we should simply become frustrated, and give up and abandon all our efforts. Instead, it should be our objective, whilst remaining within the laws of the land, to continue to remind the government of the needs of the time. We must also properly advise those groups who have vested interests, so that at a global level, justice can prevail.

Only then will we see the world become the haven of peace and harmony that we all want and desire.

Therefore, we cannot and must not give up our efforts. If we stop raising our voices against cruelty and injustice, then we will become amongst those who have no moral values or standards whatsoever. Whether or not our voices are likely to be heard or have influence is irrelevant. We must continue to counsel others towards peace. I am always extremely pleased when I see that, irrespective of differences of religion or nationality, for the sake of upholding human values, so many people come to this function to listen, to learn and to speak about ways to establish peace and compassion in the world. Thus, I would request all of you to strive for peace to the best of your abilities so that we can keep the flicker of hope alight, that a time will come when true peace and justice will be established in all parts of the world.

We must remember that when human efforts fail, then God Almighty issues His Decree to determine the fate of mankind. Before God's Decree sets into motion and compels people towards Him and towards fulfilling the rights of mankind, it would be far better if the people of the world should themselves come to pay attention to these crucial matters, because when God Almighty is forced to take action, then His Wrath seizes mankind in a truly severe and terrifying manner.

In today's world, one terrifying manifestation of God's Decree could be in the shape of another world war. There is no doubt that the effects of such a war and its destruction will not be limited to the war itself or even to this generation. In fact, its horrific consequences will be exhibited for many generations to come. Just one tragic consequence of such a war will be the effect it will have on new born children, both now and in the future. The weapons available today are so destructive that they could lead to generation after generation of children being born with severe genetic or physical defects.

Japan is the one country to have experienced the abhorrent consequences of atomic warfare, when it was attacked by nuclear bombs during the Second World War. Even today when you visit Japan and meet its people, you see an absolute fear and hatred of war visible in their eyes and from what they say. Yet the nuclear bombs that were used at that time and which caused widespread devastation, were much less powerful than the atomic weapons that are possessed by even very small nations today.

It is said that in Japan, even though seven decades have passed, yet the effects of the atom bombs are still continuing to be manifest on newborn children. If a person is shot by a bullet, then it is sometimes possible for him to survive through medical treatment, but if a nuclear war breaks out, then those who are in the firing line will have no such luck. Instead, we will find that people will instantly die and freeze like statues, and their skin will simply melt away. Drinking water, food and vegetation will all be contaminated and affected by radiation. We can only imagine what type of diseases such contamination will lead to. In those places that are not directly hit and where the effects of the radiation are somewhat less, even there the risk of diseases and illness will become much higher and the future generations will also bear much greater risks.

Therefore, as I have said, the devastating and destructive effects of such warfare will not be limited to the war and its aftermath, but will pass from generation to generation. These are the real consequences of such warfare, and yet today there are selfish and foolish people who are extremely proud of their invention and describe what they have developed as a gift to the world.

The truth is that the so-called beneficial aspects of nuclear energy and technology can be extremely dangerous and lead to widespread destruction, due to either negligence or due to accidents. We have already witnessed such catastrophes, such as the nuclear accident that occurred in 1986 in Chernobyl, in what is now Ukraine, and just last year after the earthquake and tsunami in Japan, it too had to contend with great danger and the country was placed in fear. When such events happen, then it is also very difficult to repopulate the affected regions. Due to their unique and tragic experiences, the Japanese have become extremely cautious and indeed, their sense of fear and terror is fully justified.

It is an obvious statement that people die in wars, and so when Japan entered the Second World War, its Government and its people were well-aware that some people would be killed. It is said that approximately three million people died in Japan, and this came to about 4% of the country's population. Even though a number of other countries may have suffered higher proportions of deaths in terms of total numbers, yet the hatred and aversion to war that we find in the Japanese people remains much higher in comparison to others. The simple reason for this is certainly the two nuclear bombs that were dropped on Japan during World War II, and the consequences of which they are still witnessing and having to bear even today. Japan has proved its greatness and resilience by being able to repopulate and rehabilitate its towns relatively quickly. But let it be clear that if nuclear weapons are used again today, then it is quite possible that parts of certain countries could be completely wiped off the map. They could cease to exist.

Conservative estimates put the death toll of the Second World War at about 62 million and it is said that around 40 million of those who were killed were civilians. Thus, in other words, more civilians died than military personnel. Such devastation occurred despite the fact that apart from in Japan, a traditional war was fought with conventional weapons everywhere else.

The United Kingdom had to bear the loss of around half a million people. Of course, at that time, it was still a colonial power and so its colonies also fought on its behalf. If we include their losses then the death toll rises to millions.

In India alone, around 1.6 million people lost their lives.

However, today the situation has changed, and those very countries that were colonies of the United Kingdom, and who fought for the British Empire, could today fight against Great Britain if war breaks out. Moreover, as I mentioned earlier, even some small countries have acquired nuclear weapons.

What causes great fear is the knowledge that such nuclear weapons could end up in the hands of such people who either do not have the ability or who choose not to think about the consequences of their actions. In truth, such people do not even care about the consequences, and are trigger-happy.

Thus, if the major powers do not act with justice, do not eliminate the frustrations of smaller nations and do not adopt great and wise policies, then the situation will spiral out of control and the destruction that will follow is beyond our comprehension and imagination. Even the majority of the world who do desire peace will also become engulfed by this devastation.

Thus, it is my ardent wish and hope that the leaders of all major nations come to understand this dreadful reality, and so instead of adopting aggressive policies and utilising force to achieve their aims and objectives, they strive to adopt policies that promote and secure justice.

Recently, a very senior Russian military commander issued a serious warning about the potential risk of a nuclear war. It was his view that such a war would not be fought in Asia or elsewhere, but would be fought on Europe's borders, and that the threat might originate and ignite from Eastern European countries. Though some people will say that this was simply his personal opinion, I myself do not believe his views to be improbable, but in addition, I also believe that if such a war breaks out, then it is highly likely that Asian countries will also become involved.

Another news item that was recently given widespread media coverage was the views of a recently retired chief of Israel's intelligence agency, Mossad. During an interview with the well-known American television channel, CBS, he said that it was becoming apparent that the Israeli Government wished to wage war on Iran. He said that if such an attack took place it would be impossible to know where or how such a war would come to end. Thus, he strongly advised against any attack.

In this respect, it is my opinion that such a war will end with nuclear destruction.

I recently also came across an article in which the author stated that the situation of the world today is similar to the situation in 1932, both in economic terms and also politically. He wrote that in certain countries the people held no confidence in their politicians or their so-called democracies. He also said that there were many other similarities and parallels which were combining together to form the same image today that was witnessed just prior to the outbreak of the Second World War.

Some may disagree with his analysis, but on the contrary, I agree with it and that is why I believe the world's governments ought to be extremely worried and concerned at the current state of affairs. Similarly, the unjust leaders of some Muslim countries, whose only objective is to hold onto their power at any means and at any cost, should come to their senses. Otherwise, their acts and their foolishness will be the means of their demise, and they will lead their respective countries towards a most terrifying predicament.

We, who are members of the Aḥmadiyya Muslim Community, try our utmost to save the world and humanity from destruction. This is because in this era, we have accepted the Imam of the Age, who was sent by Allah as the Promised Messiah, and came as a servant to the Holy Prophet Muhammad (peace be upon him), who himself was sent as a Mercy for all of Mankind.

It is because we follow the teachings of the Holy Prophet (peace be upon him) that we feel extreme pain and anguish in our hearts at the state of the world. It is that pain which drives us in our efforts to try and save humanity from destruction and suffering. Therefore, I and all other Ahmadi Muslims are striving to fulfil our responsibilities towards achieving peace in the world.

One way in which I have tried to promote peace is through a series of letters that I have written to certain world leaders. A few months ago, I sent a letter to Pope Benedict, which was delivered to him in person by an Ahmadi representative of mine. In the letter I said to him that as he was the leader of the world's biggest religious denomination, he ought to endeavour to establish peace.

In similar vein, more recently and upon observing that hostilities between Iran and Israel were boiling over to a very dangerous level, I sent a letter to both Israel's Prime Minister, Benjamin Netanyahu, and Iran's President, Mahmud Ahmedinejad, in which I urged them to forsake all forms of haste and recklessness when making decisions, for the sake of mankind.

I have also recently written to President Barack Obama and Canada's Prime Minister, Stephen Harper, calling on both of them to fulfil their roles and responsibilities towards the development of peace and harmony in the world.

I am also planning to write and warn other Heads of State and leaders in the near future.

I do not know if my letters will be given any value or weight by the various leaders I have written to, but whatever their reaction, an attempt has been made by me, as the Khalīfah and spiritual leader of millions of Ahmadi Muslims worldwide, to convey their feelings and emotions about the perilous state of the world.

Let it be clear that I have not expressed these sentiments because of any personal fear, but instead, I am motivated out of a sincere love for humanity.

This love for humanity has been developed and instilled in all true Muslims by the teachings of the Holy Prophet Muhammad (peace be upon him) who, as I have already mentioned, was sent as a means of mercy and compassion for all of mankind.

Most likely you will be very surprised or even shocked to hear that our love for mankind is a direct result of the teachings of the Holy Prophet (peace be upon him). The question may arise in your minds, that why then are there Muslim terrorist groups that are killing innocent people, or why are there Muslim governments, who in order to protect their seats of power, are ordering the mass killings of members of their public?

Let it be absolutely clear that in reality, such evil acts are completely contrary to the real teachings of Islam. The Holy Quran does not give permission, under any circumstances, for extremism or terrorism.

In this age, according to our beliefs, God Almighty sent the Founder of the Aḥmadiyya Muslim Jamā'at, Ḥaḍrat Mirza Ghulam Ahmad of Qadian (peace be upon him) as the Promised Messiah and the Imam Mahdi, in complete submission to the Holy Prophet Muhammad (peace be upon him). The Promised Messiah (peace be upon him) was sent to propagate the real and true teachings of Islam and the Holy Quran. He was sent to establish a bond between man and God Almighty. He was sent to identify and recognize the rights owed by man to one another. He was sent to end all forms of religious warfare. He was sent to establish the respect, dignity and honour of every Founder and every Prophet of any religion. He was sent to draw attention towards attaining the highest standards of moral values and to establish peace, love, compassion and brotherhood throughout the world.

If you go to any part of the world, you will find these very qualities embedded in all true Ahmadi Muslims. For us neither terrorists nor extremists are examples, nor are the cruel Muslim dictators examples to us, nor are Western powers examples to us. The example that we follow is that of the Founder of Islam, the Holy Prophet Muhammad (peace be upon him) and our guiding instructions are the Holy Quran.

Thus, from this Peace Symposium, I send a message to the entire world, that the message and teachings of Islam are of love, compassion, kindness and peace.

Sadly, we find that a small minority of Muslims present a completely distorted image of Islam and act upon their misguided beliefs. I say to all of you, that you should not believe this to be the real Islam and thus use such misguided acts as a licence to hurt the sentiments of the peaceful majority of Muslims or make them a target of cruelty.

The Holy Quran is the holiest and most sacred Book for all Muslims and so to use abusive and foul language or to burn it will certainly grievously injure the feelings of Muslims. We have seen that when this happens it often leads to a completely wrong and inappropriate reaction by extremist Muslims.

Just very recently we heard of two incidents in Afghanistan, where some American soldiers disrespected the Holy Quran, and killed innocent women and children in their homes. Similarly, a merciless person shot dead some French soldiers in the South of France without any reason, and then some days later he entered a school and killed three innocent Jewish children and one of their teachers.

We find that this behaviour is completely wrong and can never lead to peace. We also see such cruelties regularly come to pass in Pakistan and elsewhere and so all of these acts are giving the opponents of Islam fuel to vent their hatred and a pretext upon which to pursue their goals on a large scale. Such barbaric acts carried out on a smaller scale are not conducted due to personal enmities or grudges, but are in fact the result of the unjust policies adopted by certain governments, both at a domestic and at an international level.

Thus, for peace in the world to be established it is essential that proper standards of justice are developed at every level, and in every country of the world. The Holy Quran has deemed the killing of one innocent person without reason akin to killing all of mankind.

So once again, as a Muslim, I shall make it absolutely clear that Islam does not permit cruelty or oppression in any way, shape or form. This is an injunction that is absolute and without exception. The Quran further states that even if any country or people hold enmity towards you, that must not stop you from acting in a fully just and fair manner when dealing with them. It should not be that any enmities or rivalries lead you to taking revenge or acting disproportionately. Another vital injunction given to us by the Holy Quran is that the wealth and resources of others should not be looked upon with envy or greed.

I have mentioned just a few points, but these are such that are crucially important because they lay the foundation for peace and justice in society and the wider world. I pray that the world pays attention to these key issues, so that we can be saved from the destruction of the world that we are being led towards by the unjust and untruthful people.

I would like to take this opportunity to apologize that I have taken up quite some time, but the truth is that the subject of establishing peace in the world is of truly vast importance.

Time is running out, and before it is too late we must all pay great heed and attention to the needs of the time.

Before I bring my speech to an end, I would like to talk about one important thing. As we are all aware, these days the Diamond Jubilee of Her Majesty, Queen Elizabeth II, is being celebrated. If we rewind the clock 115 years to 1897, the Diamond Jubilee of Queen Victoria was also being celebrated. At that time, the Founder of the Aḥmadiyya Muslim Community sent a congratulatory message to Queen Victoria.

In his message, he conveyed both the teachings of Islam and he also sent a message of prayers for the British Government and for the long life of the Queen. In his message, the Promised Messiah (peace be upon him) wrote that the best quality of the Queen's Government was that under its rule, all people were granted religious freedom.

In today's world the British Government no longer rules over the Sub-Continent, but still the principles of freedom of religion are deeply entrenched in British society and its laws, through which every person is granted religious freedom.

Indeed, a very beautiful example of this freedom is being witnessed here tonight where the followers of various different faiths, religions and beliefs have joined together in one place with a common aspiration of seeking peace in the world.

Therefore, using the same words and prayers that the Promised Messiah (peace be upon him) used, I take this opportunity to offer heartfelt congratulations to Queen Elizabeth. As he said:

May our congratulations filled with happiness and gratitude to our compassionate Queen be conveyed. And may the honourable Queen always be kept happy and content.

The Promised Messiah (peace be upon him) further offered

prayers for Queen Victoria, and so again I use his words to pray for Queen Elizabeth:

> O Powerful and Noble God. Through your Grace and Blessings keep our honoured Queen forever happy in the same way that we are living happily under her benevolence and kindness; and be kind and loving to her in the same way that we are living in peace and prosperity under her generous and righteous rule.

Thus, these are sentiments of gratitude that are held by every Ahmadi Muslim who is a British citizen.

At the end I would like to once again express my gratitude to all of you from the depths of my heart, who by coming here have demonstrated their love, affection and brotherhood.

Thank you very much.

THE PATH TO PEACE—
JUST RELATIONS BETWEEN NATIONS

CAPITOL HILL
WASHINGTON, D.C., USA, 2012

Preface

On June 27, 2012, a historic event took place at Capitol Hill
in Washington, D.C. Ḥaḍrat Khalīfatul-Masīḥ V^aba, Fifth
Successor to the Promised Messiah^as and Head of the Ahmadiyya
Muslim Community, addressed leading congressmen, senators,
ambassadors, White House and State Department Staff, NGO
leaders, religious leaders, professors, policy advisors, bureaucrats,
members of the Diplomatic Corps, representatives of think-tanks
and the Pentagon and journalists from the media. The meeting,
the first of its kind, gave the opportunity to some of the most influential leaders in the United States, including Honourable Nancy
Pelosi, the Democratic Leader in the House of Representatives,
to hear first-hand Islam's message on world peace. Following the
event, His Holiness was given a tour of the Capitol Hill building, before being escorted to the House of Representatives
where a Resolution was introduced in honour of his visit to the
United States.

The introductory paragraph of the Resolution stated:

> Welcoming His Holiness, Ḥaḍrat Mirza Masroor Ahmad, the worldwide spiritual and administrative head of the Ahmadiyya Muslim Community, to Washington, DC, and recognizing his commitment to world peace, justice, nonviolence, human rights, religious freedom and democracy...

The full list of attendees at the Capitol Hill event reads as follows:

- U.S. Senator Robert Casey, Sr. (Democrat Pennsylvania)
- U.S. Senator John Cornyn (Republican Texas)
- Democratic Leader Nancy Pelosi (Democrat California)
- U.S. Congressman Keith Ellison (Democrat Minnesota)
- U.S. Congressman Bradley Sherman (Democrat California)
- U.S. Congressman Frank Wolf (Republican Virginia)
- U.S. Congressman Michael Honda (Democrat California)
- U.S. Congressman Timothy Murphy (Republican Pennsylvania)
- U.S. Congresswoman Jeannette Schmidt (Republican Ohio)
- U.S. Congresswoman Janice Hahn (Democrat California)
- U.S. Congresswoman Janice Schakowsky (Democrat Illinois)
- U.S. Congresswoman Jackie Speier (Democrat California)
- U.S. Congresswoman Zoe Lofgren (Democrat California)

- U.S. Congresswoman Sheila Jackson Lee (Democrat Texas)

- U.S. Congressman Gary Peters (Democrat Michigan)

- U.S. Congressman Thomas Petri (Republican Wisconsin)

- U.S. Congressman Adam Schiff (Democrat California)

- U.S. Congressman Michael Capuano (Democrat Massachusetts)

- U.S. Congressman Howard Berman (Democrat California)

- U.S. Congresswoman Judy Chu (Democrat California)

- U.S. Congressman André Carson (Democrat Indiana)

- U.S. Congresswoman Laura Richardson (Democrat California

- U.S. Congressman Lloyd Poe (Republican Texas)

- U.S. Congressman Barney Frank (Democrat Massachusetts)

- U.S. Congressman. Bruce Braley (Democrat Iowa)

- U.S. Congressman Dennis Kucinich (Democrat Ohio)

- U.S. Congressman Trent Franks (Republican Arizona)

- U.S. Congressman Chris Murphy (Democrat Connecticut)

- U.S. Congressman Hank Johnson (Democrat Georgia)

- U.S. Congressman James Clyburn (Democrat South Carolina)

- His Excellency Bockari Kortu Stevens, Ambassador of Sierra Leone to the United States

- Dr. Katrina Lantos Swett, Chairwoman, United States Commission on Inteternational Religious Freedom

- Hon. Tim Kaine, Former Governor of Virginia

- Amb. Susan Burk, Special Representative of President Barack Obama for Nuclear Nonproliferation

- Amb. Suzan Johnson Cook, U.S. Ambassador at Large for International Religious Freedom

- Hon. Khaled Aljalahma, Deputy Chief of Mission, Embassy of the Kingdom of Bahrain to the United States

- Rev. Monsignor Jean-Francois Lantheaume, First Counselor (Deputy Chief of Mission), The Apostolic Nunciature of the Holy See to the United States

- Ms. Sara Al-Ojaili, Public Affairs/Liaison Officer, Embassy of the Sultanate of Oman to the United States

- Mr. Salim Al Kindie, First Secretary, Embassy of the Sultanate of Oman to the United States

- Ms. Fozia Fayyaz, Embassy of Pakistan to the United States

- Hon. Saida Zaid, Counselor, Embassy of Morocco to the United States

- Hon. Nabeel Munir, Minister-IV (Security Council), Pakistan Permanent Mission to the United Nations

- Hon. Josef Renggli, Minister-Counselor, Embassy of Switzerland to the United States

- Hon. Alyssa Ayres, Deputy Assistant Secretary for South and Central Asia, U.S. Department of State

- Amb. Karl Inderfurth, Senior Adviser and Wadhwani Chair in U.S.-India Policy Studies, Center for Strategic and International Studies

- Hon. Donald A. Camp, Senior Associate, Center for Strategic and International Studies
- Amb. Jackie Wolcott, Executive Director, U.S. Commission on International Religious Freedom
- Dr. Azizah al-Hibri, Commissioner, U.S. Commission on International Religious Freedom
- Mr. Isaiah Leggett, County Executive, Montgomery Count, Maryland
- Ms. Victoria Alvarado, Director, Office of International Religious Freedom, U.S. Department of State
- Dr. Imad Dean Ahmad, Director, Minaret of Freedom Institute
- Dr. Zainab Alwani, Assistant Professor of Islamic Studies, Howard University School of Divinity
- Ms. Deborah L. Benedict, Associate Counsel, U.S. Citizenship and Immigration Services, Department of Homeland Security
- Ms. Lora Berg, Senior Adviser to Special Representative to Muslim Communities, U.S. Department of State
- Dr. Charles Butterworth, Professor (Emeritus) of Government and Politics, University of Maryland, College Park
- Father John Crossin, Executive Director for Secretariat for Ecumenical and Interreligious Affairs, United States Conference of Catholic Bishops
- Major (Ret.) Franz Gayl, Senior Science Adviser, U.S. Marine Corps.

- Dr. Sue Gurawadena-Vaughn, Director of International Religious Freedom and South East Asia Programs, Freedom House

- Mr. Frank Jannuzi, Head of Washington Office, Amnesty International USA

- Mr. T. Kumar, International Advocacy Director, Amnesty International USA

- George Leventhal, Member of the Montgomery County Council

- Mr. Amer Latif, Visiting Fellow, Wadhwani Chair in U.S.-India Policy Studies, Center for Strategic and International Studies

- Mr. Tim Lenderking, Director of Pakistan Desk Office, U.S. State Department

- Mr. Jalal Malik, International Affairs Officer, U.S. Army National Guard

- Mr. Naveed Malik, Foreign Service Officer, U.S. Department of State

- Ms. Dalia Mogahed, Senior Analyst and Executive Director, Gallup Center for Muslim Studies

- Mr. Paul Monteiro, Associate Director, White House Office of Public Engagement

- Major General David Quantock, United States Army Provost General

- Ms. Tina Ramirez, Director of International and Government Relations, The Becket Fund

- Rabbi David Saperstein, Director and Counsel, Religious Action Center for Reform Judaism

- Chaplain, Brigadier General Alphonse Stephenson, Director of the National Guard Bureau Office of the Chaplain
- Mr. Knox Thames, Director of Policy and Research, U.S. Commission on International Religious Freedom
- Mr. Eric Treene, Special Counsel for Religious Discrimination, Civil Rights Division, U.S. Department of Justice
- Dr. Hassan Abbas, Professor, Regional and Analytical Studies Department, National Defense University
- Mr. Malik Siraj Akbar, Reagan-Fascell Fellow, National Endowment of Democracy
- Mr. Matthew K. Asada, Congressional Fellow to Rep. Gary Peters
- Ms. Stacy Burdett, Director of Government and National Affairs, Anti-Defamation League
- Ms. Elizabeth Cassidy, Deputy Director for Policy and Research, U.S. Commission on International Religious Freedom
- Ms. Aimee Chiu, Director of Media, Communication, and Public Relations, American Islamic Congress
- Mr. Cornelius Cremin, Department of State, Bureau of Democracy, Human Rights and Labor, Acting Deputy Director and Foreign Affairs Officer for Pakistan
- Mr. Sadanand Dhume, Resident Fellow, American Enterprise Institute
- Dr. Richard Gathro, Dean of Nyack College, Washington D.C.

- Mr. Joe Grieboski, Chairman, The Institute on Religion and Public Policy

- Ms. Sarah Grieboski, The Institute on Religion and Public Policy

- Dr. Max Gross, Adjunct Professor, Prince Alwaleed Bin Talal Center for Muslim-Christian Understanding, Georgetown University

- Dr. Riaz Haider, Clinical Professor of Medicine, George Washington University

- Ms. Huma Haque, Assistant Director, South Asia Center, Atlantic Council

- Mr. Jay Kansara, Associate Director, Hindu American Foundation

- Mr. Hamid Khan, Senior Program Officer, Rule of Law Center, U.S. Institute for Peace

- Ms. Valerie Kirkpatrick, Associate for Refugees and U.S. Advocacy, Human Rights Watch

- Mr. Alex Kronemer, Unity Productions

- Mr. Paul Liben, Executive Writer, U.S. Commission on International Religious Freedom

- Ms. Amy Lillis, Foreign Affairs Officer, U.S. Department of State

- Mr. Graham Mason, Legislative Assistant to Rep. Allyson Schwartz

- Ms. Lauren Markoe, Religion News Service

- Mr. Dan Merica, CNN.com

- Mr. Joseph V. Montville, Senior Associate, Merrimack

College Center for the Study of Jewish-Christian-Muslim Relations

- Mr. Aaron Myers, Program Officer, Freedom House
- Ms. Attia Nasar, Regional Coordinating Officer, U.S. Department of State
- Ms. Melanie Nezer, Senior Director, US Policy and Advocacy, HIAS
- Dr. Elliott Parris, Bowie State University
- Mr. John Pinna, Director of Government and International Relations, American Islamic Congress
- Mr. Arif Rafiq, Adjunct Scholar, Middle East Institute
- Ms. Maya Rajaratnam, Amnesty International
- Ms. Rachel Sauer, Foreign Affairs Officer, U.S. Department of State
- Dr. Jerome Schiele, Dean of College of Professional Studies, Bowie State University
- Ms. Samantha Schnitzer, Staff, United States Commission on International Religious Freedom
- Dr. Mary Hope Schwoebel, Senior Program Officer, Academy for International Conflict Management and Peacebuilding, U.S. Institute for Peace
- Ms. Sarah Schlesinger, International and Government Relations Associate, The Becket Fund
- Dr. Frank Sellin, Kyrgystan Desk Officer, U.S. Department of State
- Ms. Anna-Lee Stangl, Christian Solidarity Worldwide

- Ms. Kalinda Stephenson, Professional Staff, Tom Lantos Human Rights Commission

- Mr. Jordan Tama, Lead Democratic Staffer, Tom Lantos Human Rights Commission

- Mr. Shaun Tandon, AFP

- Dr. Wilhelmus Valkenberg, Professor of Religion and Culture, The Catholic University of America

- Mr. Anthony Vance, Director of External Affairs, Baha'is of the United States

- Mr. Jihad Saleh Williams, Government Affairs Representative, Islamic Relief USA

- Ms. Amelia Wang, Chief of Staff to Congresswoman Judy Chu

- Ms. Moh Sharma, Legislative Fellow to Congresswoman Judy Chu

U.S. Congress—House Resolution 709

IV

112TH CONGRESS
2D SESSION

H. RES. 709

Welcoming His Holiness, Hadhrat Mirza Masroor Ahmad, the worldwide spiritual and administrative head of the Ahmadiyya Muslim Community, to Washington, DC, and recognizing his commitment to world peace, justice, nonviolence, human rights, religious freedom, and democracy.

IN THE HOUSE OF REPRESENTATIVES

JUNE 27, 2012

Ms. ZOE LOFGREN of California (for herself, Mr. SHERMAN, Mr. CONNOLLY of Virginia, Mr. HINCHEY, Ms. ESHOO, Ms. SPEIER, Ms. RICHARDSON, Mr. SCHIFF, Ms. SCHAKOWSKY, Mr. HONDA, Mr. WOLF, Mr. PETERS, Mr. DENT, Ms. CHU, Mr. BERMAN, Mr. FRANKS of Arizona, Ms. JACKSON LEE of Texas, Ms. SCHWARTZ, Mr. BRALEY of Iowa, and Mr. McGOVERN) submitted the following resolution; which was referred to the Committee on Foreign Affairs

RESOLUTION

Welcoming His Holiness, Hadhrat Mirza Masroor Ahmad, the worldwide spiritual and administrative head of the Ahmadiyya Muslim Community, to Washington, DC, and recognizing his commitment to world peace, justice, nonviolence, human rights, religious freedom, and democracy.

Whereas, from June 16, 2012, to July 2, 2012, His Holiness, Hadhrat Mirza Masroor Ahmad, the worldwide spiritual and administrative head of the Ahmadiyya Muslim Community, an international religious organization with mil-

2

lions of members across the globe, is making a historic
visit to the United States;

Whereas His Holiness was elected to become fifth Khalifa to
Mirza Ghulam Ahmad, a lifelong position, on April 22,
2003;

Whereas His Holiness is a leading Muslim figure promoting
peace, who in his sermons, lectures, books, and personal
meetings has continually advocated the Ahmadiyya values
of service to humanity, universal human rights, and a
peaceful and just society;

Whereas the Ahmadiyya Muslim Community has suffered re-
peated hardships, including discrimination, persecution,
and violence;

Whereas, on May 28, 2010, 86 Ahmadi Muslims were killed
in Lahore, Pakistan, when two mosques belonging to the
Ahmadiyya Muslim Community were attacked by anti-
Ahmadiyya terrorists;

Whereas despite the continued sectarian persecution that
Ahmadi Muslims are subjected to, His Holiness continues
to forbid violence;

Whereas His Holiness has traveled globally to promote and
facilitate service to humanity, meeting with presidents,
prime ministers, parliamentarians, and ambassadors of
state;

Whereas during his visit to the United States, His Holiness
will meet thousands of American Muslims in addition to
significant United States Government leaders in order to
strengthen relationships and find means of establishing
peace and justice for all people; and

Whereas, on the morning of June 27, 2012, His Holiness will
deliver the keynote address at a special bipartisan recep-

•HRES 709 IH

3

tion at the Rayburn House Office Building on Capitol
Hill, "The Path to Peace: Just Relations Between Nations": Now, therefore, be it

1   *Resolved*, That the House of Representatives—

2   (1) welcomes His Holiness, Mirza Masroor

3   Ahmad to Washington, DC;

4   (2) commends His Holiness for promoting indi-

5   vidual and world peace, as well as individual and

6   world justice; and

7   (3) commends His Holiness for his perseverance

8   in counseling Ahmadi Muslims to eschew any form

9   of violence, even in the face of severe persecution.

○

The Path to Peace—Just Relations Between Nations

Bismillāhir-Raḥmānir-Raḥīm—In the name of Allah, the Gracious, Ever Merciful.

All distinguished guests—*assalāmu ʿalaikum wa raḥmatullāhe wa barakātohū*—peace and blessings of Allah be upon you all.

Before proceeding, I would like to first of all take this opportunity to thank you all for taking the time to come and listen to what I have to say. I have been requested to speak about a subject that is extremely vast and wide ranging. It has many different aspects and therefore, it is not possible for me to cover all of them in the short time available. The subject that I have been asked to speak about is the establishment of world peace. Certainly, this is the most vital and pressing issue facing the world today. However, as the time is limited, I will only briefly give the Islamic viewpoint on the establishment of peace through just and equal relations between nations.

The truth is that peace and justice are inseparable—you cannot have one without the other. Certainly, this principle is something that all wise and intelligent people understand. Leaving aside those people who are determined to create disorder in the world, no one can ever claim that in any society, country or even the entire world, that there can be disorder or a lack of peace where justice and fair dealing exist. Nevertheless, we find in many parts of the world that disorder and a lack of peace are prevalent. Such disorder is visible both internally within countries, and externally in terms of the relations between various nations. Such disorder and strife exists even though all governments claim to make policies that are based on justice. All claim that the establishment of peace is their primary objective. Yet, in general, there is little doubt that restlessness and anxiety is increasing in the world, and so disorder is spreading. This clearly proves that somewhere along the line, the requirements of justice are not being fulfilled. Therefore, there is an urgent need to try and end inequality, wherever and whenever it exists. Thus, as the worldwide Head of the Ahmadiyya Muslim Community, I would like to make a few observations about the need for, and the ways to achieve peace based on justice.

The Ahmadiyya Muslim Community is purely a religious community. It is our firm belief that the Messiah and Reformer who was destined to appear in this age and enlighten the world as to Islam's true teachings has indeed arrived. We believe that the Founder of our Community, Ḥaḍrat Mirza Ghulam Ahmad[as] of Qadian, was that very Promised Messiah and Reformer, and thus we have accepted him. He pressed upon his followers to act and propagate the real and true teachings of Islam that are based on the Holy Quran. Therefore, everything that I will say in relation to establishing peace, and in relation to conducting just international relations, will be based on Quranic teachings.

In relation to achieving world peace, all of you regularly express your opinions, and indeed make great efforts. Your creative and intelligent minds allow you to present great ideas, plans and indeed a vision of peace. Thus, this issue does not require me to speak from a worldly or political perspective, but instead my entire focus will be based on how to establish peace based on religion. For this purpose I shall, as I have earlier said, present some very important guidelines based on the teachings of the Holy Quran.

It is important to always remember that human knowledge and intellect is not perfect, but is in fact limited. Thus, when making decisions or forming thoughts often certain factors enter human minds, which can cloud judgement and lead to a person trying to fulfil his own rights. Ultimately, this can lead to an unjust outcome and decision being made. God's Law, however, is perfect and so no vested interests or unfair provisions exist. This is because God only desires for the good and betterment of His Creation and therefore, His Law is based entirely on justice. The day the people of the world come to recognise and understand this crucial point will be the day that the foundation for true and everlasting peace will be laid. Otherwise, we continue to find that although efforts are endlessly made to establish world peace, yet they are unable to provide any worthwhile results.

After the conclusion of the First World War, the leaders of certain countries desired for good and peaceful relations between all nations in future. Thus, in an effort to achieve world peace the League of Nations was formed. Its principal aim was to maintain world peace and to prevent future wars from breaking out. Unfortunately, the rules of the League and the resolutions it passed had certain flaws and weaknesses and so they did not properly protect the rights of all peoples and all nations equally. Consequently, as a result of the inequalities that existed, long-term peace could not prevail. The efforts of the League failed and this led directly to World War II.

We are all aware of the unparalleled destruction and devastation that ensued, where around 75 million people globally lost their lives, many of who were innocent civilians. That war should have been more than enough to open the eyes of the world. It should have been a means to developing wise policies that granted all parties their due rights, based on justice, and thus prove to be a means of establishing peace in the world. The world's governments at the time did endeavour to some extent to try and establish peace, and hence the United Nations was established. However, it soon became quite apparent that the noble and over-arching objective underpinning the United Nations could not be fulfilled. Indeed, today certain governments quite openly make statements that prove its failure.

What does Islam say in relation to international relations that are based on justice, and so a means of establishing peace? In the Holy Quran, God Almighty has made it clear that whilst our nationalities or ethnic backgrounds act as a means of identity, they do not entitle or validate any form of superiority of any kind.[*]

The Quran, thus, makes clear that all people are born equal. Furthermore, in the final sermon ever delivered by the Holy Prophet Muhammad[sa], he instructed all Muslims to always

---

[*]   ch. 49: v. 14

remember that an Arab is not superior to a non-Arab and nor is a non-Arab superior to an Arab. He taught that a white person is not superior to a black person and nor is a black person superior to a white person. Thus, it is a clear teaching of Islam that the people of all nationalities and all races are equal. It is also made clear that all people should be granted equal rights without any discrimination or prejudice. This is the key and golden principle that lays the foundation for harmony between different groups and nations, and for the establishment of peace.

However, today we find that there is division and separation between powerful and weaker nations. For example, in the United Nations we find that there is a distinction made between certain countries. Thus, in the Security Council there are some permanent members and some non-permanent members. This division has proved to be an internal source of anxiety and frustration and thus we regularly hear reports of certain countries protesting against this inequality. Islam teaches absolute justice and equality in all matters and so we find another very crucial guideline in Chapter 5, verse 3 of the Holy Quran. In this verse it states that to fully comply with the requirements of justice, it is necessary to treat even those people, who go beyond all limits in their hatred and enmity, with fairness and equity. The Quran teaches that wherever and whoever counsels you towards goodness and virtue, you should accept it, and wherever and whoever counsels you towards sinful or unjust behaviour, you should reject it.

A question that naturally arises is that what is the standard of justice required by Islam? In Chapter 4, verse 136, the Holy Quran states that even if you have to testify against yourself, or your parents or your most loved ones, then you must do so in order to uphold justice and to uphold the truth. Powerful and rich countries should not usurp the rights of the poor and weaker countries in an effort to preserve their own rights, and nor should they deal with the poorer nations in an unjust fashion. On the other hand, the poor and weaker nations should not seek to inflict harm on the powerful or wealthy nations whenever the opportunity arises. Instead, both sides should endeavour to fully abide by the principles of justice. Indeed, this is a matter of crucial importance in maintaining peaceful relations between countries.

Another requirement for peace between nations based on justice is given in Chapter 15, verse 89 of the Holy Quran where it states that no party should ever look enviously at the resources and wealth of others. Similarly, no country should seek to unjustly appropriate or take over the resources of another country on the false pretext of trying to assist or support them. Thus, on the basis of providing technical expertise, governments should not take advantage of other nations by making unjust trade deals or contracts. Similarly, on the basis of providing expertise or assistance, governments should not try to take control of the natural resources or assets of the developing nations. Where less educated people or governments need to be taught how to properly utilise their natural resources, then this should be done.

Then, nations and governments should always seek to serve and help those less fortunate. However, such service should not be rendered with an aim of achieving national or political benefits or as a means to fulfil vested interests. We find that in the past six or seven decades the United Nations has launched many programmes or foundations aiming to help the poor countries to progress. Towards this effort they have explored the natural resources of the developing nations. However, despite these efforts, none of the poorer countries have reached the stage or level of the developed nations. One reason for this is certainly wide-ranging corruption by many of the governments of those under-developed countries. With regret though I must say that despite this, as a means to further their own interests, the developed nations have continued to deal with such governments. Trade deals, international aid and business contracts have continued to be processed. As a result, the frustrations and restlessness of the poor and deprived segments of society have continued to increase and this has led to rebellion and internal disorder within those countries. The poor people of the developing countries have become so frustrated that they have turned against not only their own leaders, but also the big powers as well. This has played into the hands of the extremist groups, who have taken advantage of the frustrations, and so have been able to encourage such people towards joining their groups and supporting their hate-filled ideology. The ultimate result of this has been that the peace of the world has been destroyed.

Thus, Islam has drawn our attention to various means for peace. It requires absolute justice. It requires truthful testimony to always be given. It requires that our glances are not cast enviously in the direction of the wealth of others. It requires that the developed nations put aside their vested interests, and instead help and serve the less developed and poorer nations with a truly selfless attitude and spirit. If all of these factors are observed, then true peace will be established.

If despite all these aforementioned measures any country transgresses all limits and attacks another country, and seeks to unjustly take control of its resources, then other countries should certainly take measures to stop such cruelty—but they should always act with justice when doing so.

The circumstances for taking action, based on Islamic teachings are detailed in the Quran, in Chapter 49.* It teaches that when two nations are in dispute and this leads to war, then other governments should strongly counsel them towards dialogue and diplomacy so that they can come to an agreement and reconciliation on the basis of a negotiated settlement. If, however, one of the parties does not accept the terms of agreement and wages war, then other countries should unite together and fight to stop that aggressor. When the aggressive nation is defeated and agrees to mutual negotiation, then all parties should work towards an agreement that leads to long-standing peace and reconciliation. Harsh and unjust conditions should not be enforced that leads to the hands of any nation being tied, because in the long-term that will lead to restlessness, which will ferment and spread. The result of such restlessness will be further disorder.

In circumstances where a third-party government seeks to bring about reconciliation between two parties, then it should act with sincerity and total impartiality. This impartiality should remain even if one of the parties speaks against it. Therefore, the third-party should display no anger in such circumstances, it should seek no revenge, nor should it act in an unfair manner. All parties should be afforded their due rights.

Thus, for the requirements of justice to be fulfilled, it is essential that the countries that are negotiating a settlement should themselves not seek to fulfil their own personal interests, nor try

---

* ch. 49: v.10

to derive benefit unduly from either country. They should not interfere unjustly or pressure either of the parties unfairly. The natural resources of any country should not be taken advantage of. Unnecessary and unfair restrictions should not be placed upon such countries, because this is neither just and nor can it ever prove to be a source of improving relations between countries.

Due to time constraints, I have only very briefly mentioned these points. In short, if we desire for peace to be established in the world, then we must leave aside our personal and national interests for the greater good and instead we must establish mutual relations that are based entirely on justice. Otherwise, some of you might agree with me that due to alliances, blocs may be formed in future—or I can even say they have started forming—and it is not unlikely that disorder will continue to increase in the world, which will ultimately lead to a huge destruction. The effects of such devastation and warfare will surely last for many generations. Therefore, the United States, as the world's largest power, should play its role in acting with true justice and with such good intentions, as I have described. If it does so then the world will always remember with great admiration your great efforts. It is my prayer that this becomes a reality.

Thank you very much. Thank you again.

According our tradition, at the end of the function we normally perform a silent prayer. Thus, I will perform the silent prayer and the Ahmadis will follow me. All of you, our guests, can pray in your own way.

LETTERS
TO
THE WORLD LEADERS

LETTER TO HIS HOLINESS POPE BENEDICT THE XVI

MIRZA MASROOR AHMAD
HEAD OF THE AHMADIYYA COMMUNITY
IN ISLAM

16 Gressenhall Road,
London,
SW18 5QL,
UK

31 October 2011

To His Holiness Pope Benedict the XVI,

It is my prayer that may Allah the Almighty bestow His Grace and Blessings upon you.

As Head of the worldwide Ahmadiyya Muslim Community, I convey to His Holiness the Pope the message of the Holy Qur'an: Say, *'O People of the Book! come to a word equal between us and you—that we worship none but Allah, and that we associate no partner with Him, and that some of us take not others for Lords beside Allah.'*

Islam, nowadays, is under the glare of the world, and is frequently targeted with vile allegations. However, those raising these allegations do so without studying any of Islam's real teachings. Unfortunately, certain Muslim organisations due only to their vested interests, have portrayed Islam in a totally wrong light. As a result, distrust has increased in the hearts of the people of Western and non-Muslim countries towards Muslims, to the extent that even otherwise extremely well-educated people make baseless allegations against the Founder of Islam, the Holy Prophet Muhammad(pbuh).

The purpose of every religion has been to bring man closer to God and to establish human values. Never has the founder of any religion taught that his followers should usurp the rights of others or should act cruelly. Thus, the actions of a minority of misguided Muslims should not be used as a pretext to attack Islam and its Holy Founder(pbuh). Islam teaches us to respect the Prophets of all religions and this is why it is essential for a Muslim to believe in all of the prophets who are mentioned in the Holy Bible or in the Holy Qur'an, until and including Jesus Christ(pbuh). We are the humble servants of the Holy Prophet Muhammad(pbuh) and so we are deeply grieved and saddened by the attacks on our Holy Prophet(pbuh); but we respond by continuing to present his noble qualities to the world and to disclose even more of the beautiful teachings of the Holy Qur'an.

If a person does not follow a particular teaching properly whilst claiming to subscribe to it, then it is he who is in error, not the teaching. The meaning of the word 'Islam' itself means peace, love and security. *There should be no compulsion in matters of faith* is a clear injunction of the Qur'an. From cover to cover, the Holy Qur'an teaches love, affection, peace, reconciliation and the spirit of sacrifice. The Holy Qur'an states repeatedly that one who does not adopt righteousness is far removed from Allah, and therefore, is far removed from the teachings of Islam. Hence, if anybody portrays Islam as an extreme and violent religion filled with teachings of bloodshed, then such a portrayal has no link with the real Islam.

The Ahmadiyya Muslim Community practises only the true Islam and works purely to please God Almighty. If any Church or other place of worship stands in need of protection, they will find us standing shoulder to shoulder with them. If any message resonates from our mosques it will only be that of Allah is Great and that we bear witness that there is none worthy of worship except Him and Muhammad(pbuh) is the Messenger of Allah.

A factor playing a major role in destroying the peace of the world is that some people perceive that as they are intelligent, well-educated and liberated, they are free to ridicule and mock founders of religions. To maintain peace in society it is necessary for one to eliminate all sentiments of hostility from one's heart and to increase one's levels of tolerance. There is a need to stand in defence of the respect and reverence of each other's Prophets. The world is passing through restlessness and unease and this requires that by creating an atmosphere of love and affection, we remove this anxiety and fear; that we convey a message of love and peace to those around; that we learn to live with ever greater harmony and in a way better than before; and that we recognise the values of humanity.

Today, small-scale wars are erupting in the world, while in other places, the superpowers are claiming to try and bring about peace. It is no longer a secret that on the surface we are told one thing, but behind the scenes their real priorities and policies are secretly being fulfilled. Can peace in the world be established in such circumstances is the question. It is with regret that if we now observe the current circumstances of the world closely, we find that the foundation for another world war has already been laid. If after the Second World War a path of equity leading to justice was followed, we would not witness the current state of the world, whereby it has again become engulfed in the flames of war. As a consequence of so many countries having nuclear weapons, grudges and enmities are increasing and the world sits on the precipice of destruction. If these weapons of mass destruction explode, many future generations will never forgive us for having inflicted permanent disabilities upon them. There is still time for the world to pay attention to the rights of the Creator and of His Creatures.

I believe that now, rather than focusing on the *progress* of the world, it is more important, indeed it is essential, that we urgently increase our efforts to *save* the world from this destruction. There is an urgent need for mankind to recognise its Creator as this is the only guarantor for the survival of humanity; otherwise, the world is rapidly moving towards self-destruction. If today man really wants to be successful in establishing peace, then instead of finding fault with others, he should try to control the Satan within. By removing his own evils, a person should present a wonderful example of justice. I frequently remind the world that these excessive enmities towards others are completely usurping human values and so are leading the world towards obliteration.

As you have an influential voice in the world, I urge you to also inform the wider world that by placing obstacles in the way of the natural balance established by God, they are moving rapidly towards annihilation. This message needs to be conveyed further and wider than ever before and with much greater prominence.

All the religions of the world are in need of religious harmony and all the people of the world need a spirit of love, affection and brotherhood to be created. It is my prayer that we all understand our responsibilities and play our role in establishing peace and love, and for the recognition of our Creator in the world. We ourselves have prayer, and we constantly beseech Allah that may this destruction of the world be avoided. I pray that we are saved from the destruction that awaits us.

Yours sincerely,

Mirza Masroor Ahmad
Khalifatul Masih V
Head of the worldwide
Ahmadiyya Muslim Community

LETTER TO THE PRIME MINISTER
OF ISRAEL

نَحْمَدُهُ وَنُصَلِّى عَلَى رَسُوْلِهِ الْكَرِيْمِ

وعلى عبدِهِ الْمَسِيح الْمَوعود

خدا کے فضل اور رحم کے ساتھ

هو الناصر

MIRZA MASROOR AHMAD
HEAD OF THE AHMADIYYA COMMUNITY
IN ISLAM

16 Gressenhall Road
Southfields, London
SW18 5QL, UK

26 February 2012

His Excellency
Mr Benjamin Netanyahu
Prime Minister of Israel
Jerusalem

Dear Prime Minister,

I recently sent a letter to His Excellency Shimon Peres, President of Israel, regarding the perilous state of affairs emerging in the world. In light of the rapidly changing circumstances, I felt it was essential for me to convey my message to you also, as you are the Head of the Government of your country.

The history of your nation is closely linked with prophethood and Divine revelation. Indeed, the Prophets of the Children of Israel made very clear prophecies regarding your nation's future. As a result of disobedience to the teachings of the Prophets and negligence towards their prophecies, the Children of Israel had to suffer difficulties and tribulations. If the leaders of your nation had remained firm in obedience to the Prophets, they could have been saved from enduring various misfortunes and adversities. Thus, it is your duty, perhaps even more so than others, to pay heed to the prophecies and injunctions of the Prophets.

I address you as the Khalifa of that Promised Messiah and Imam Mahdi (peace be upon him), who was sent as the servant of the Holy Prophet Muhammad (peace and blessings of Allah be upon him); and the Holy Prophet (peace and blessings of Allah be upon him) was sent as the Mercy for All Mankind amongst the brethren of the Children of Israel in the semblance of Moses (peace be upon him) (Deuteronomy, 18:18). Hence, it is my duty to remind you of God's Message. I hope that you will come to be counted amongst those who hearken to God's Call, and who successfully find the right path; that path which is in accordance with the Guidance of God the Supreme, the Master of the heavens and the earth.

We hear reports in the news nowadays that you are preparing to attack Iran. Yet the horrific outcome of a World War is right before you. In the last World War, whilst millions of other people were killed, the lives of hundreds of thousands of Jewish persons were also wasted. As the Prime Minister, it is your duty to protect the life of your nation. The current circumstances of the world indicate that a World War will not be fought between only two countries, rather blocs will come into formation. The threat of a World War breaking out is a very serious one. The life of Muslims, Christians and Jews are all at peril from it. If such a war occurs, it will result in a chain reaction of human destruction. The effects of this catastrophe will be felt by future generations, who will either be born disabled, or crippled. This is because undoubtedly, such a war will involve atomic warfare.

Hence, it is my request to you that instead of leading the world into the grip of a World War, make maximum efforts to save the world from a global catastrophe. Instead of resolving disputes with force, you should try to resolve them through dialogue, so that we can gift our future generations with a bright future rather than 'gift' them with disability and defects.

I shall try to elucidate my views based on the following passages from your teachings, the first extract being from the Zabur:

'Do not fret because of evil-doers. Do not envy those who do wrong. For they shall soon be cut down like the grass, and wither like the green herb. Trust in God, and do good. Dwell in the land, and enjoy safe pasture. Also delight yourself in God, and he will give you the desires of your heart. Commit your way to God. Trust also in him, and he will do this: He will make your righteousness go forth as the dawn, and your justice as the noon day sun. Rest in God, and wait patiently for him. Do not fret because of him who prospers in his way, because of the man who makes wicked plots happen. Cease from anger, and forsake wrath. Do not fret, it leads only to evildoing. For evildoers shall be cut off, but those who wait for God shall inherit the land. For yet a little while, and the wicked will be no more. Yes, though you look for his place, he is not there. But the humble shall inherit the land, and shall delight themselves in the abundance of peace.' (Zabur, 37:1-11).

Similarly, we find in the Torah:

'Thou shalt not have in thy bag divers weights, a great and a small. Thou shalt not have in thine house divers measures, a great and a small. [But] thou shalt have a perfect and just weight, a perfect and just measure shalt thou have: that thy days may be lengthened in the land which the LORD thy God giveth thee. For all that do such things, [and] all that do unrighteously, [are] an abomination unto the LORD thy God.' (Deuteronomy, 25:13-16).

Thus, world leaders, and particularly you should terminate the notion of governance by force and should refrain from oppressing the weak. Instead, strive to spread and promote justice and peace. By doing so, you will remain in peace yourselves, you will gain strength and world peace will also be established.

It is my prayer that you and other world leaders understand my message, recognise your station and status and fulfil your responsibilities.

Yours Sincerely,

MIRZA MASROOR AHMAD
Khalifatul Masih V
Head of the Worldwide
Ahmadiyya Muslim Community

LETTER TO THE PRESIDENT OF
THE ISLAMIC REPUBLIC OF IRAN

نَحْمَدُه وَ نُصَلِّى عَلَى رَسُوْلِهِ الْكَرِيْمِ

وعلى عبده المسيح الموعود

خدا کے فضل اور رحم کے ساتھ

هو الناصر

MIRZA MASROOR AHMAD
HEAD OF THE AHMADIYYA COMMUNITY
IN ISLAM

16 Gressenhall Road
Southfields, London
SW18 5QL, UK

His Excellency
President of the Islamic Republic of Iran
Mahmoud Ahmadinejad
Tehran

7 March 2012

Dear Mr President,

Assalamo Alaikum Wa Rahmatullahe Wa Barakatohu,

In light of the perilous state of affairs emerging in the world, I felt that it was essential for me to write to you, as you are the President of Iran, and thus you hold the authority to make decisions which will affect the future of your nation and the world at large. There is currently great agitation and restlessness in the world. In some areas small-scale wars have broken out, while in other places the superpowers act on the pretext of trying to bring about peace. Each country is engaged in activities to either help or oppose other countries, but the requirements of justice are not being fulfilled. It is with regret that if we now observe the current circumstances of the world, we find that the foundation for another world war has already been laid. As so many countries, both large and small, have nuclear weapons, grudges and hostilities are increasing. In such a predicament, the Third World War looms almost certainly before us. As you are aware, the availability of nuclear weapons will mean that a Third World War will be an atomic war. Its ultimate result will be catastrophic, and the long term effects of such warfare could lead to future generations being born disabled or deformed.

It is my belief that as followers of the Holy Prophet Muhammad[pbuh], who was sent to establish peace in the world, and who was the *Rahmatulil Aalameen* – the Mercy to all of Mankind –we do not and cannot desire for the world to suffer such a fate. This is why my request to you is that as Iran is also a significant power in the world, it should play its role to prevent a Third World War. It is undeniably true that the major powers act with double standards. Their injustices have caused restlessness and disorder to spread all across the world. However, we cannot ignore the fact that some Muslim groups act inappropriately, and contrary to the teachings of Islam. Major world powers have used this as a pretext to fulfil their vested interests by taking advantage of the poor Muslim countries. Thus, I request you once again, that you should focus all of your efforts and energies towards saving the world from a Third World War. The Holy Qur'an teaches Muslims that enmity against any nation should not hinder them from acting in a just manner. In *Surah Al Mai'dah*, Allah the Exalted instructs us:

"And let not the enmity of a people, that they hindered you from the Sacred Mosque, incite you to transgress. And help one another in righteousness and piety; but help not one

another in sin and transgression. And fear Allah; surely, Allah is severe in punishment." (Ch.5:V.3)

Similarly, in the same chapter of the Holy Qur'an we find the following commandment to Muslims:

"O ye who believe! Be steadfast in the cause of Allah, bearing witness in equity; and let not a people's enmity incite you to act otherwise than with justice. Be always just, that is nearer to righteousness. And fear Allah. Surely, Allah is aware of what you do." (Ch.5:V.9)

Hence, you should not oppose another nation merely out of enmity and hatred. I admit that Israel exceeds beyond its limits, and has its eyes cast upon Iran.
Indeed, if any country transgresses against your country, naturally you have the right to defend yourself. However, as far as possible, disputes should be resolved through diplomacy and negotiations. This is my humble request to you, that rather than using force, use dialogue to try and resolve conflicts. The reason why I make this request is because I am the follower of that Chosen Person of God who came in this era as the True Servant of the Holy Prophet Muhammad(pbuh), and who claimed to be the Promised Messiah and Imam Mahdi. His mission was to bring mankind closer to God and to establish the rights of people in the manner our Master and Guide, the *Rahmatullil Aalameen* – the Mercy to all of Mankind – the Holy Prophet(pbuh) demonstrated to us. May Allah the Exalted enable the Muslim *Ummah* to understand this beautiful teaching.

Wassalam,
Yours Sincerely,

MIRZA MASROOR AHMAD
Khalifatul Masih V
Head of the Worldwide
Ahmadiyya Muslim Community

LETTER TO THE PRESIDENT OF THE UNITED STATES OF AMERICA

MIRZA MASROOR AHMAD
HEAD OF THE AHMADIYYA COMMUNITY
IN ISLAM

16 Gressenhall Road
Southfields, London
SW18 5QL, UK

President Barack Obama
President of the United States of America
The White House
1600 Pennsylvania Avenue NW
Washington D.C.

8 March 2012

Dear Mr President,

In light of the perturbing state of affairs developing in the world, I felt that it was necessary for me to write to you, as you are the President of the United States of America, a country which is a world superpower, and thus you hold the authority to make decisions which will affect the future of your nation and the world at large.

There is currently great agitation and restlessness in the world. Small-scale wars have broken out in certain areas. Unfortunately, the superpowers have not been as successful as was anticipated in their efforts to establish peace in these conflict-hit regions. Globally, we find that almost every country is engaged in activities to either support, or oppose other countries; however, the requirements of justice are not being fulfilled. It is with regret that if we now observe the current circumstances of the world, we find that the foundation for another world war has already been laid. As so many countries, both large and small, have nuclear weapons, grudges and hostilities are increasing between nations. In such a predicament, the Third World War looms almost certainly before us. Such a war would surely involve atomic warfare; and therefore, we are witnessing the world head towards a terrifying destruction. If a path of equity and justice had been followed after the Second World War, we would not be witnessing the current state of the world today whereby it has become engulfed in the flames of war once again.

As we are all aware, the main causes that led to the Second World War were the failure of League of Nations and the economic crisis, which began in 1932. Today, leading economists state that there are numerous parallels between the current economic crisis and that of 1932. We observe that political and economic problems have once again led to wars between smaller nations, and to internal discord and discontentment becoming rife within these countries. This will ultimately result in certain powers emerging to the helm of government, who will lead us to a world war. If in the smaller countries conflicts cannot be resolved through politics or diplomacy, it will lead to new blocs and groupings to form in the world. This will be the precursor for the outbreak of a Third World War. Hence, I believe that now, rather than focusing on the *progress* of the world, it is more important and indeed essential, that we urgently increase our efforts to *save* the world from this destruction. There is an urgent need for mankind to recognise its One God, Who is our Creator, as this is the only guarantor for the survival of humanity; otherwise, the world will continue to rapidly head towards self-destruction.

My request to you, and indeed to all world leaders, is that instead of using force to suppress other nations, use diplomacy, dialogue and wisdom. The major powers of the world, such as the United States, should play their role towards establishing peace. They should not use the acts of smaller countries as a pretext to disturb world harmony. Currently, nuclear arms are not only possessed by the United States and other major powers; rather, even relatively smaller countries now possess such weapons of mass destruction, where those who are in power are often trigger-happy leaders who act without thought or consideration. Thus, it is my humble request to you to strive to your utmost to prevent the major and minor powers from erupting into a Third World War. There should be no doubt in our minds that if we fail in this task then the effects and aftermath of such a war will not be limited to only the poor countries of Asia, Europe and the Americas; rather, our future generations will have to bear the horrific consequences of our actions and children everywhere in the world will be born disabled or deformed. They will never forgive their elders who led the world to a global catastrophe. Instead of being concerned for only our vested interests, we should consider our coming generations and strive to create a brighter future for them. May God the Exalted enable you, and all world leaders, to comprehend this message.

Yours Sincerely,

MIRZA MASROOR AHMAD
Khalifatul Masih V
Head of the Worldwide
Ahmadiyya Muslim Community

LETTER TO THE
PRIME MINISTER OF CANADA

MIRZA MASROOR AHMAD
HEAD OF THE AHMADIYYA COMMUNITY
IN ISLAM

16 Gressenhall Road
Southfields, London
SW18 5QL, UK

Mr Stephen Harper
Prime Minster of Canada
Ottawa, Ontario

8 March 2012

Dear Prime Minister,

In light of the dire state of affairs developing in the world, I felt that it was necessary for me to write to you, as you are the Prime Minister of Canada, and hence you hold the authority to make decisions which will affect the future of your nation and the world at large. There is currently great agitation and restlessness in the world. Small-scale wars have broken out in certain areas. Unfortunately, the superpowers have not been as successful as was anticipated in their efforts to establish peace in these conflict-hit regions. Globally, we find that almost every country is engaged in activities to either support, or oppose other countries; however, the requirements of justice are not being fulfilled. It is with regret that if we now observe the current circumstances of the world, we find that the foundation for another world war has already been laid. As so many countries, both large and small, have nuclear weapons, grudges and hostilities are increasing between nations. In such a predicament, the Third World War looms almost certainly before us. Such a war would surely involve atomic warfare; and therefore, we are witnessing the world head towards a terrifying destruction. If a path of equity and justice had been followed after the Second World War, we would not be witnessing the current state of the world today whereby it has become engulfed in the flames of war once again.

As we are all aware, the main causes that led to the Second World War were the failure of League of Nations and the economic crisis, which began in 1932. Today, leading economists state that there are numerous parallels between the current economic crisis and that of 1932. We observe that political and economic problems have once again led to wars between smaller nations, and to internal discord and discontentment becoming rife within these countries. This will ultimately result in certain powers emerging to the helm of government, who will lead us to a world war. If in the smaller countries conflicts cannot be resolved through politics or diplomacy, it will lead to new blocs and groupings to form in the world. This will be the precursor for the outbreak of a Third World War. Hence, I believe that now, rather than focusing on the *progress* of the world, it is more important and indeed essential, that we urgently increase our efforts to *save* the world from this destruction. There is an urgent need for mankind to recognise its One God, Who is our Creator, as this is the only guarantor for the survival of humanity; otherwise, the world will continue to rapidly head towards self-destruction.

Canada is widely considered to be one of the most just countries in the world. Your nation does not normally interfere in the internal problems of other countries. Further, we, the Ahmadiyya Muslim Community, have special ties of friendship with the people of Canada. Thus, I request you to strive to your utmost to prevent the major and minor powers from leading us into a devastating Third World War.

My request to you, and indeed to all world leaders, is that instead of using force to suppress other nations, use diplomacy, dialogue and wisdom. The major powers of the world, such as Canada, should play their role towards establishing peace. They should not use the acts of smaller countries as a pretext to disturb world harmony. Currently, nuclear arms are not only possessed by the major world powers, rather even relatively smaller countries now possess such weapons of mass destruction; where those who are in power are often trigger-happy leaders who act without thought or consideration. Thus, it is my humble request to you that use all your energy and efforts to prevent a Third World War from occurring. There should be no doubt in our minds that if we fail in this task then the effects and aftermath of such a war, will not be limited to only the poor countries of Asia, Europe and the Americas; rather, our future generations will have to bear the horrific consequences of our actions and children everywhere in the world will be born disabled or deformed. They will never forgive their elders who led the world to a global catastrophe. Instead of being concerned for only our vested interests, we should consider our coming generations and strive to create a brighter future for them. May God the Exalted enable you, and all world leaders, to comprehend this message.

Yours Sincerely,

MIRZA MASROOR AHMAD
Khalifatul Masih V
Head of the Worldwide Ahmadiyya Muslim Community

LETTER TO THE CUSTODIAN OF THE TWO HOLY PLACES THE KING OF THE KINGDOM OF SAUDI ARABIA

نَحْمَدُهُ وَ نُصَلِّى عَلٰى رَسُوْلِهِ الْكَرِيْمِ

وعلٰى عبده المسيح الموعود

خدا کے فضل اور رحم کے ساتھ

هو النّاصِرُ

MIRZA MASROOR AHMAD
HEAD OF THE AHMADIYYA COMMUNITY
IN ISLAM

16 Gressenhall Road
Southfields, London
SW18 5QL, UK

28 March 2012

Custodian of the Two Holy Places
King of the Kingdom of Saudi Arabia
Abdullah bin Abdul-Aziz Al Saud
Riyadh, Saudi Arabia

Respected King Abdullah,

Assalamo Alaikum Wa Rahmatullahe Wa Barakatohu,

Today, I am writing to you with the intention of raising a most important matter, because as the Custodian of the Two Holy Places and the King of Saudi Arabia, you hold a very high station in the Muslim *Ummah.* For located within your country are the two holiest sites in Islam—Makkah Al-Mukarramah and Madinah Al-Munawwarah—which to love constitutes a part of the faith of Muslims. These sites are also the centres of spiritual progress for and are greatly revered by Muslims. In this light, all Muslims and Muslim governments confer special status upon you. This status requires that on the one hand, you should properly guide the Muslim *Ummah* and on the other, you should strive to create an atmosphere of peace and harmony within Muslim countries. You should also endeavour to develop mutual love and sympathy between Muslims and to enlighten them regarding the essence of:

رُحَمَاءُ بَيْنَهُمْ

Ultimately, you should strive to create peace in the entire world for the benefit of all of mankind. As Head of the Ahmadiyya Muslim Jama'at and the Khalifa of the Promised Messiah and Imam Mahdi (peace be upon him), it is my request that, irrespective of certain doctrinal disagreements that exist between the Ahmadiyya Muslim Jama'at and other sects of Islam, we should still unite in an effort to establish world peace. We should do our level best to educate the world regarding the true teachings of Islam, which are based on love and peace. By doing so, we can dispel the misconceptions in general that are embedded in the people of the West and the world about Islam. Enmity against other nations or groups should not hinder us from acting in a just manner. Allah the Almighty states in Verse 3 of *Surah Al-Ma'idah* of the Holy Qur'an:

وَلَا يَجْرِمَنَّكُمْ شَنَاٰنُ قَوْمٍ اَنْ صَدُّوْكُمْ عَنِ الْمَسْجِدِ الْحَرَامِ اَنْ تَعْتَدُوْا وَتَعَاوَنُوْا عَلَى الْبِرِّ وَالتَّقْوٰى

وَلَا تَعَاوَنُوْا عَلَى الْاِثْـمِ وَالْعُدْوَانِ وَاتَّقُوا اللّٰهَ اِنَّ اللّٰهَ شَدِيْدُ الْعِقَابِ ۞

'.... And let not the enmity of a people, that they hindered you from the Sacred Mosque, incite you to transgress. And help one another in righteousness and piety; but help not one another in sin and transgression. And fear Allah; surely, Allah is severe in punishment.'

This is the guiding principle that we should keep in view so that we can fulfil our duty to present the beautiful image of Islam to the world. It is with sentiments of heartfelt love and deep compassion for all Muslims worldwide that I am requesting you to play your role in this regard.

We find in the world today that some politicians and so-called scholars are planting seeds of hatred against Islam in an attempt to defame the Holy Prophet (peace be upon him). They try to present completely distorted interpretations of the teachings of the Holy Qur'an to achieve their aims. Further, the conflict between Palestine and Israel is worsening every day and hostilities between Israel and Iran have heightened to such an extent that their relationship has severely broken down. Such circumstances require that as an extremely important leader in the Muslim *Ummah*, you should make every effort to resolve these disputes with justice and equality. The Ahmadiyya Muslim Jama'at does everything it possibly can to dispel the hatred against Islam, wherever and whenever it surfaces. Until the entire Muslim *Ummah* unites as one and makes efforts towards this, peace can never be established.

Thus, it is my request to you to do your utmost in this regard. If World War III is indeed destined to occur, at least we should strive to ensure that it does not originate from any Muslim country. No Muslim country or any Muslim individual anywhere in the world, today or in the future, will want to shoulder the blame for being the spark for a global catastrophe, the long-term effects of which will lead to future generations being born with defects or deformities, for if a World War breaks out now, it will surely be fought with nuclear weapons. We have already experienced just a glimpse of the utter devastation caused by atomic warfare when nuclear bombs were dropped on two cities in Japan during World War II.

Thus, O King of Saudi Arabia! Expend all your energy and influence to save the world from annihilation! May Allah the Almighty provide you with His Help and Succour, *Amin*. With prayers for you and for the entire Muslim *Ummah* of:

اِهْدِنَا الصِّرَاطَ الْمُسْتَقِيْمَ ۝

Wassalam,
Yours Sincerely,

MIRZA MASROOR AHMAD
Khalifatul Masih V
Head of the worldwide
Ahmadiyya Muslim Community

LETTER TO THE PREMIER OF THE STATE COUNCIL OF THE PEOPLE'S REPUBLIC OF CHINA

MIRZA MASROOR AHMAD
HEAD OF THE AHMADIYYA COMMUNITY
IN ISLAM

16 Gressenhall Road
Southfields, London
SW18 5QL

His Excellency,
Premier of the State Council of the People's Republic of China
Mr Wen Jiabao
Zhongnanhai, China

9 April 2012

Dear Premier,

I am sending this letter to you through one of our representatives of the Ahmadiyya Muslim Community. He is the President of our Community in Kababir, Israel and was invited by the Minister for Minorities in China. Our representative was introduced to Chinese officials during a visit by a delegation from China, which included the Deputy Minister for Minorities, to our Mission House in Kababir.

The Ahmadiyya Muslim Community is that sect in Islam which firmly believes that the Messiah and Reformer, who was destined to appear in this age as the Mahdi for the guidance of Muslims, as the Messiah for the guidance of Christians and as a guide for the reformation of all mankind, has indeed arrived in accordance with the prophecies of the Holy Prophet Muhammad (peace be upon him), and thus we have accepted him. His name was Hadhrat Mirza Ghulam Ahmad (peace be upon him) from Qadian, India. In accordance with God Almighty's command, he laid the foundation for the Ahmadiyya Muslim Community in 1889. By the time he passed away in 1908, hundreds of thousands of people had joined the fold of the Community. After his demise, the institution of Khilafat was established. Currently, we are in the era of the 5th Khilafat, and I am the 5th Khalifa of the Promised Messiah (peace be upon him).

An extremely important and fundamental aspect of our teaching is that in this era religious wars should come to an end. Further, we believe that anyone who desires to convey or spread any teaching should only do so in a spirit and atmosphere of love, compassion and brotherhood so that he can become the source of establishing peace, reconciliation and harmony. This important aspect, which is based on the true teachings of Islam, is being promoted and propagated by the Ahmadiyya Muslim Community all over the world. The Community is now spread over 200 countries of the world, and consists of millions of followers.

I wish to convey the following message to you: that the world is currently passing through a most harrowing and perilous period. Indeed, it would appear that we are rapidly drawing closer to a world war. You are the leader of a great superpower. In addition, an enormous proportion of the world's population live under your governance. You also possess the right to use the power to veto when required in the United Nations. Hence, in this context, it is my request to you to play your role to save the world from the destruction that looms before us. Irrespective of nationality, religion, caste or creed, we should strive to our utmost to save humanity.

In China, after the revolution took place, there was great progress and change. Honourable Mao Zedong, who was a great leader of your nation, established the foundation for high moral standards, which can also be described in other words as the most excellent standard of human values. Although you do not believe in the existence of God and your principles are based on morality, I would like to make it clear that our God, Who is the God as portrayed by Islam, revealed the Qur'an as guidance for all mankind, and the Qur'an inculcates all such morals that you act upon, but it is also filled with even further moral guidance. It contains beautiful teachings expounding the means of sustenance for humanity and establishing human values. If the world—the Muslim world in particular—adopt these Qur'anic teachings, all problems and conflicts will be resolved and an atmosphere of peace and harmony will be fostered.

Today, the Ahmadiyya Muslim Community endeavours to further this very purpose and objective in every part of the world. Through our peace symposiums and through numerous meetings that I hold with various categories of people and groups from all walks of life, I remind the world of this vital goal. It is my prayer that the leaders of the world act with wisdom and do not allow mutual enmities between nations and people on a small-scale to erupt into a global conflict. It is also my request to you that, as a great superpower of the world, play your role to establish world peace. Save the world from the horrifying consequences of a world war, for if such a war breaks out, it will come to an end with the use of atomic weapons. It is quite possible that as a result, parts of certain countries and areas of the world will be obliterated off the face of the earth. The effects and aftermath of an atomic war will not be limited to just the immediate devastation, rather, the long-term effects will result in future generations being born disabled or with defects. Thus, expend all your energy, capabilities and resources in the effort to save humanity from such dreadful consequences. It will ultimately be to the benefit of your nation to act upon this. It is my prayer that all countries of the world, large and small, come to understand this message.

With best wishes and prayers,

Yours Sincerely,

MIRZA MASROOR AHMAD
Khalifatul Masih V
Head of the worldwide
Ahmadiyya Muslim Community

LETTER TO THE PRIME MINISTER
OF THE UNITED KINGDOM

نَحْمَدُهُ وَ نُصَلِّى عَلَى رَسُوْلِهِ الْكَرِيْم
وعلى عبدِهِ الْمَسِيح الْمَوعود
خدا کے فضل اور رحم کے ساتھ
هو الناصر

MIRZA MASROOR AHMAD
HEAD OF THE AHMADIYYA COMMUNITY
IN ISLAM

16 Gressenhall Road
Southfields, London
SW18 5QL
United Kingdom

15 April 2012

Prime Minister of the United Kingdom of
Great Britain and Northern Ireland
Rt. Hon. David Cameron
10 Downing Street, London
SW1A 2AA
United Kingdom

Dear Prime Minister,

In light of the perilous and precarious circumstances that the world is currently passing through, I felt it necessary to write to you. As the Prime Minister of the United Kingdom, you have the authority to make decisions that will affect the future of your country, and the world at large. Today, the world stands in dire need of peace because the sparks of war can be seen all around the world. Conflicts between countries on a small-scale are threatening to erupt into a global conflict. We observe that the situation of the world today is similar to the situation in 1932, both economically and politically. There are many other similarities and parallels, which when combined together, form the same image today that was witnessed just prior to the outbreak of the Second World War. If these sparks ever truly ignite, we will witness the terrifying scenario of a Third World War. With numerous countries, large and small, possessing nuclear weapons, such a war would undoubtedly involve atomic warfare. The weapons available today are so destructive that they could lead to generation after generation of children being born with severe genetic or physical defects. Japan is the one country to have experienced the abhorrent consequences of atomic warfare, when it was attacked by nuclear bombs during the Second World War, annihilating two of its cities. Yet the nuclear bombs that were used at that time and which caused widespread devastation, were much less powerful than the atomic weapons that are possessed by even certain small nations today. Therefore, it is the duty of the superpowers to sit down together to find a solution to save humanity from the brink of disaster.

What causes great fear is the knowledge that the nuclear weapons in smaller countries could end up in the hands of trigger-happy people who either do not have the ability, or who choose not to think about the consequences of their actions. If the major powers do not act with justice, do not eliminate the frustrations of smaller nations and do not adopt great and wise policies, then the situation will spiral out of all control and the destruction that will follow is beyond our comprehension and imagination. Even the majority of the world's population who do desire peace will also become engulfed by this devastation.

Thus, it is my ardent wish and prayer that you and the leaders of all major nations come to understand this dreadful reality, and so instead of adopting aggressive policies and utilising force to achieve your aims and objectives, you should strive to adopt policies that promote and secure justice.

If we look at the recent past, Britain ruled over many countries and left behind a high standard of justice and religious freedom, especially in the Sub-Continent of India and Pakistan. When the Founder of the Ahmadiyya Muslim Community congratulated Her Majesty, Queen Victoria, on her Diamond Jubilee and conveyed to her the message of Islam, he especially prayed for God to generously reward the British Government due to the manner in which it governed justly and with equity. He greatly praised the British Government for its just policies and for granting religious freedom. In today's world, the British Government no longer rules over the Sub-Continent, but still principles of freedom of religion are deeply entrenched in British society and its laws, through which every person is granted religious freedom and equal rights. This year the Diamond Jubilee of Her Majesty, Queen Elizabeth II, is being celebrated, which gives Britain an opportunity to demonstrate its standards of justice and honesty to the world. The history of the Ahmadiyya Muslim Community demonstrates that we have always acknowledged this justice whenever displayed by Britain and we hope that in future also, justice will remain a defining characteristic of the British Government, not only in religious matters, but in every respect that you will never forget the good qualities of your nation from the past and that in the current world situation, Britain will play its role in establishing peace worldwide.

It is my request that at every level and in every direction we must try our level best to extinguish the flames of hatred. Only if we are successful in this effort, will we be enabled to guarantee brighter futures for our generations to come. However, if we fail in this task, there should be no doubt in our minds that as result of nuclear warfare, our future generations everywhere will have to bear the horrific consequences of our actions and they will never forgive their elders for leading the world into a global catastrophe. I again remind you that Britain is also one of those countries that can and does exert influence in the developed world as well as in developing countries. You can guide this world, if you so desire, by fulfilling the requirements of equity and justice. Thus, Britain and other major powers should play their role towards establishing world peace. May God the Almighty enable you and other world leaders to understand this message.

With best wishes and with prayers,

Yours Sincerely,

MIRZA MASROOR AHMAD
Khalifatul Masih V
Head of the worldwide
Ahmadiyya Muslim Community

LETTER TO THE CHANCELLOR
OF GERMANY

نَحْمَدُه وَ نُصَلِّى عَلى رَسُوْلِهِ الْكَرِيْمِ
وعَلى عبدهِ الْمَسِيحِ الْمَوعود

خدا کے فضل اور رحم کے ساتھ

هو الناصــــر

MIRZA MASROOR AHMAD
HEAD OF THE AHMADIYYA COMMUNITY
IN ISLAM

16 Gressenhall Road
Southfields, London
SW18 5QL
United Kingdom

15 April 2012

Her Excellency
Chancellor of Germany
Angela Merkel
Bundeskanzleramt
Willy-Brandt-Str.1
10557 Berlin

Dear Chancellor,

In light of the alarming and extremely worrying state of affairs in the world today, I considered it necessary to write to you. As the Chancellor of Germany, a country which has significant power and influence in the world, you have the authority to make decisions that will affect your country and the entire world. Today, when the world is becoming divided into blocs, extremism is escalating and the financial, political and economic situation is worsening, there is an urgent need to extinguish all kinds of hatred and to lay the foundation for peace. This can only be achieved by respecting all of the sentiments of each and every person. However, as this is not being implemented properly, honestly and with virtue, the world situation is rapidly spiralling out of control. We observe that the requirements of justice are not being fulfilled by most nations, and as a result, the foundation for another World War has already been laid. Numerous countries, both large and small, now possess nuclear weapons. Thus, if a World War now breaks out, it is likely that it will not be fought with conventional weapons; rather, it will be fought with atomic weapons. The destruction that will result from a nuclear conflict will be utterly devastating. Its effects will not be limited to only the immediate aftermath; rather future generations will suffer from the long-term effects and will be born with serious medical and genetic defects.

Thus, it is my belief that to establish world peace, true justice is required, and the sentiments and the religious practices of all people should be honoured. I appreciate that many Western countries have generously permitted the people of poor or under-developed nations to settle in their respective countries, amongst whom are Muslims as well. Undoubtedly, there is a minority of so-called Muslims who act completely inappropriately and create distrust in the hearts of the people of the Western nations. However, it should be clear that their acts have no link with Islam whatsoever. Such extremists do not truly love the Holy Prophet Muhammad (peace be upon him), who brought a message of peace, love and reconciliation to the world. Indeed, the actions of just a handful of misguided people should not be used as a basis to raise objections against our religion and to hurt the sentiments of the majority of sincere and innocent Muslims. Peace in society is a two-way process and can only be established if all parties work together towards mutual reconciliation. Due to the mistrust in the hearts of the people in the West, instead of relationships between nations and people improving, the reaction of some non-Muslims is getting worse by the day and is creating a chasm between the Muslim and non-Muslim world.

We observe that on the basis of the misguided acts of certain Muslim groups and nations, the vested interests of some of the major powers are given preference to honesty and justice. Some of the powerful countries of the world desire to maintain easy access to the wealth and resources of certain countries and wish to avoid competing countries from having complete access to these same resources. That is why decisions are often made on the basis of helping people, or establishing world peace. Further, a major factor underlying the current political circumstances in the world is the economic downturn, which is pulling us towards another World War. If truth was truly being exhibited then some of these countries would derive benefit from each other in a just manner, by forming proper industrial and economic ties, based on fair dealings. They would not try to derive illegitimate benefit from the resources of one another, but instead would seek to come together and mutually assist one another. In short, the disorder prevalent in the world today is based upon one overriding factor, and that is a complete lack of justice, which is causing widespread anxiety and restlessness.

Thus, it is my request that strive to your utmost to prevent a World War from breaking out. Utilise all your energy, resources and influence to save the world from the horrific destruction that looms before us. According to reports, Germany will be providing three advanced submarines to Israel which could be armed with nuclear weapons. One German Professor has stated that such a decision will only serve to flare up the already heightened tensions between Israel and Iran. We must remember that nuclear weapons are not possessed by only the major powers of the world; rather, even relatively smaller countries now possess nuclear weapons. What is worrying is that in some of these small countries the leaders are trigger-happy, and appear unconcerned of the consequences of using such weapons. Therefore, once again, it is my humble request to you that try your level best to establish world peace. If we fail in this task there should be no doubt in our minds that a nuclear conflict will cause devastation that will lead to generation after generation being born with defects, and who will never forgive their elders for leading us into a global catastrophe. May God the Almighty enable you, and all world leaders, to understand this message.

With best wishes and with prayers,

Yours Sincerely,

MIRZA MASROOR AHMAD
Khalifatul Masih V
Head of the worldwide
Ahmadiyya Muslim Community

LETTER TO THE PRESIDENT OF
THE FRENCH REPUBLIC

MIRZA MASROOR AHMAD
HEAD OF THE AHMADIYYA COMMUNITY
IN ISLAM

نَحْمَدُهُ وَ نُصَلِّي عَلَى رَسُوْلِهِ الْكَرِيْمِ

وعَلَى عبدِهِ الْمَسِيحِ الْمَوْعُود

خدا کے فضل اور رحم کے ساتھ

هُوَالنَّاصِـــرُ

16 Gressenhall Road
Southfields, London
SW18 5QL
United Kingdom

15 April 2012

President of the French Republic
His Excellency Nicolas Sarkozy
Palais de l'Elysee
55, Rue du Faubourg Saint-Honore
75008 Paris
France

Dear Mr President,

In light of the rapidly changing circumstances in the world, I considered it necessary for me to write to you, because as the President of France, you have the authority to make decisions that will affect your nation, and the world at large. I believe that the world's governments ought to be extremely concerned at the current state of affairs in the world. Injustices and hostilities between nations are threatening to boil over into a global conflict. During the last century, two World Wars were fought. After the First World War, the League of Nations was established, however, the requirements of justice were not fulfilled and consequently, this led to the Second World War, culminating in the use of atom bombs. Subsequently, the United Nations was established for the protection of human rights and to maintain global peace. Thus, the means for avoiding wars were considered, yet today we observe that the foundation for a Third World War has already been laid. Numerous countries, both small and large, possess atom bombs. What is worrying is that some of the smaller nuclear powers are irresponsible and ignorant about the devastating consequences of such weapons. It is not inconceivable that if nuclear weapons are used, the horrific aftermath will become immediately manifest and that day will be like Doomsday. The weapons available today are so destructive that they could lead to generation after generation of children being born with severe genetic or physical defects. It is said that in Japan, the one country to have experienced the devastating destruction of atomic warfare, even though seven decades have passed, the effects of the atom bombs are still continuing to be manifest on newborn children.

Thus, it is my humble request that strive to your utmost to extinguish the enmities and mistrust between the Muslim and non-Muslim world. Some European countries hold significant reservations regarding the teachings and traditions of Islam and have placed certain restrictions on them, whilst others are considering how to do so. The animosity that some extremist so-called Muslims already hold towards the West might lead them to reacting in an inappropriate manner, which would lead to further religious intolerance and dissention. Islam, however, is a peace-loving religion, which does not teach us to do wrong to stop something wrong. We, the Ahmadiyya Muslim Community, follow this principle and believe in peaceful solutions to all matters.

Sadly, we find that a small minority of Muslims present a completely distorted image of Islam and act upon their misguided beliefs. I say out of love for the Holy Prophet Muhammad (peace be upon him), who was the *'Mercy for all Mankind'*, that you should not believe this to be the real Islam and thus use such misguided acts as a licence to hurt the sentiments of the peaceful majority of Muslims. Recently, a merciless and heartless person shot dead some French soldiers in the South of France for no reason, and then some days later, he entered a school and killed three innocent Jewish children and one of their teachers. We also see such cruelties regularly come to pass in other Muslim countries and so all of these acts are giving the opponents of Islam fuel to vent their hatred and a basis upon which to pursue their goals on a large scale. As a Muslim, I shall make it absolutely clear that Islam does not permit cruelty or oppression in any way, shape or form. The Holy Qur'an has deemed the killing of one innocent person without reason akin to killing all mankind. This is an injunction that is absolute and without exception. The Qur'an further states that even if any country or people hold enmity towards you that must not stop you from acting in a fully just and fair manner when dealing with them. Enmities or rivalries should not lead you to taking revenge, or to acting disproportionately. If you desire conflicts to be resolved in the best manner, endeavour to search for amicable solutions. I appreciate that many Western countries have generously permitted the people of poor or under-developed nations to settle in their respective countries, amongst whom are Muslims as well. Indeed, many Muslims live in your country and thus are also your citizens. The majority are law-abiding and sincere. Moreover, Islam clearly states that love for one's country is part of the faith. The Ahmadiyya Muslim Community acts and promotes this message throughout the world. This is my message to you also, that if this true teaching of Islam is spread everywhere, then the requirements of showing love to one's nation and peace, will remain established within each country and between countries of the world.

My humble request to you, and indeed to all world leaders, is that instead of using force to suppress other nations, use diplomacy, dialogue and wisdom. The major powers of the world, such as France, should play their role towards establishing peace. They should not use the acts of smaller countries as a basis to disturb world harmony. Thus, I again remind you to strive to your utmost to prevent the major and minor powers from erupting into a Third World War. There should be no doubt in our minds that if we fail in this task then the effects and aftermath of such a war will not be limited to only the poor countries of Asia, Europe and the Americas; rather, our future generations will have to bear the horrific consequences of our actions and children everywhere in the world will be born with defects. It is my prayer that the leaders of the world act with wisdom and do not allow mutual enmities between nations and people on a small-scale to erupt into a global conflict. May God the Exalted enable you, and all world leaders, to comprehend this message.

With best wishes and with prayers,

Yours Sincerely,

MIRZA MASROOR AHMAD
Khalifatul Masih V
Head of the worldwide
Ahmadiyya Muslim Community

LETTER TO HER MAJESTY
THE QUEEN OF
THE UNITED KINGDOM AND
COMMONWEALTH REALMS

نَحْمَدُهُ وَ نُصَلِّى عَلٰى رَسُوْلِهِ الْكَرِيْمِ

وعلٰى عبده المسيح الموعود

خدا کے فضل اور رحم کے ساتھ

هوالناصـــر

MIRZA MASROOR AHMAD
HEAD OF THE AHMADIYYA COMMUNITY
IN ISLAM

16 Gressenhall Road
Southfields, London
SW18 5QL
United Kingdom

19 April 2012

Her Majesty, Queen Elizabeth II
Queen of the United Kingdom and Commonwealth Realms
Buckingham Palace
London, SW1A 1AA
United Kingdom

Your Majesty,

As Head of the Ahmadiyya Muslim Community, and on behalf of the millions of members of the Ahmadiyya Muslim Community worldwide, I express my heartfelt congratulations to Her Majesty, the Queen, on the joyous occasion of the Diamond Jubilee. We are exceptionally grateful to God the Almighty for enabling us to partake in this glorious celebration. In particular, all Ahmadi Muslims who are citizens of the United Kingdom take great pleasure and pride in the occasion of the Diamond Jubilee. Therefore, on their behalf, I convey sincere and heartfelt congratulations to Her Majesty. May God the Exalted keep our generous Queen perpetually in happiness and contentment.

I beseech the Noble God, Who created the heavens and the earth and filled them with countless blessings for our sustenance, that May He always grant our Queen, whose generous rule comprises many sovereign states and commonwealth nations, with peace, tranquillity and security. Just as Her Majesty is loved and respected by all her subjects, old and young, it is our prayer that Her Majesty comes to be loved by the Angels of God. May the All-Powerful and Mighty God shower Her Majesty generously with His countless spiritual bounties and blessings, just as He has granted her with worldly blessings in abundance. Through these blessings, may all citizens of this great nation be enabled to recognise the Supreme Lord and come to live in mutual love and affection. Irrespective of colour, creed, nationality or religion may all citizens of the United Kingdom show respect and honour to one another, to such a degree, that the positive impact and influence of this attitude extends beyond these shores and spreads to the people of other countries of the world also. May the world, much of which today is embroiled in wars, disorder and enmities instead become a haven of peace, love, brotherhood and friendship. It is my strong belief that the vision and efforts of Her Majesty can play a prominent role towards achieving this critical and overarching objective.

In the last century, two World Wars were fought in which millions of lives were lost. If today grievances between nations continue to increase, it will ultimately lead to the outbreak of another World War. The likely use of nuclear weapons in a World War will mean that the world will witness untold and horrifying destruction. May God prevent such a catastrophe from occurring and may all people of the world adopt wisdom and sense. It is my humble request to Her Majesty to use the joyous celebration of the Diamond Jubilee, as a favour to mankind, to remind all people that all nations, whether large or small, should come to live in mutual love, peace and harmony.

In this context, on the auspicious occasion of the Diamond Jubilee, I would also humbly request Her Majesty to give the world the message that the followers of any religion, and even those who do not believe in God, should always respect the sentiments of the people of any other faith. Today, misconceptions regarding Islam are prevalent in the world. This on the one hand wounds the sentiments of peace-loving Muslims, whilst on the other, develops contempt and mistrust against Islam in the hearts of non-Muslims. Thus, it will be an act of great kindness and a favour to the followers of all religions, and indeed the entire world, if Her Majesty counsels all people to be respectful to religions and their followers. May the Noble Lord provide His Help and Succour to our Queen in the fulfilment of this objective.

As I mentioned at the beginning of this letter, I am the Head of the worldwide Ahmadiyya Muslim Community. In this regard, I would like to provide a very brief overview of our Community. The Ahmadiyya Muslim Community firmly believes that the Promised Messiah and Reformer who, according to the prophecies of the Holy Prophet Muhammad (peace be upon him) and past Prophets was destined to appear in this age, is none other than Hadhrat Mirza Ghulam Ahmad of Qadian (peace be upon him). In 1889, he founded a pure and righteous community—the Ahmadiyya Muslim Community. His purpose for forming this Community was to establish a relationship between man and God and to incline people towards fulfilling the rights of one another so that they can live in mutual respect, and in goodwill. When Hadhrat Mirza Ghulam Ahmad (peace be upon him) passed away in 1908, he had approximately 400,000 followers. After his demise, the system of Khilafat was established in accordance with the Divine Will and currently, this humble servant of God is the Fifth Khalifa of the Promised Messiah (peace be upon him). Thus, the Ahmadiyya Muslim Community endeavours to further the mission of its Founder throughout the world. Our message is one of love, reconciliation and brotherhood and our motto is 'Love for All, Hatred for None'. Indeed, this embodies the beautiful teachings of Islam in a nutshell.

It would be pertinent to mention here that it is a pleasant coincidence that during the era of the Founder of the Ahmadiyya Muslim Community, the Diamond Jubilee of Her Majesty, Queen Victoria, was celebrated. At the time, the Founder of the Ahmadiyya Community wrote a book, called *A Gift for the Queen*, in which he wrote a message of congratulations to Queen Victoria. In his message, Hadhrat Mirza Ghulam Ahmad (peace be upon him) congratulated the Queen on her Diamond Jubilee, and for the manner in which all subjects under her rule, including the people of the Sub-Continent of India, were provided with justice and religious freedom and lived in peace. He presented the beautiful teachings of Islam and elucidated the purpose of his advent and claim. Although the people of the Sub-Continent have now been granted independence by the British Government, the fact that in Britain the Government has allowed people of diverse backgrounds and religions to live here, and has granted them all equal rights, freedom of religion and freedom to express and to propagate their beliefs, is ample proof of Britain's very high levels of tolerance.

Today, there are thousands of Ahmadi Muslims living in the United Kingdom. Many of them have fled here to seek refuge from the persecution they faced in their own countries. Under the generous rule of Her Majesty, they enjoy a peaceful life in which they receive justice, and freedom of religion. For this generosity, I would like to once again express my gratitude from my heart to our noble Queen.

I shall conclude my letter with the following prayer for Her Majesty, which is virtually the same prayer that was offered by the Founder of the Ahmadiyya Muslim Community for Her Majesty, Queen Victoria:

"O Powerful and Noble God! Through your Grace and Blessings keep our honoured Queen forever joyful, in the same way that we are living joyfully under her benevolent and benign rule. Almighty God! Be kind and loving to her, in the same way that we are living in peace and prosperity under her generous and kind rule."

Further, it is my prayer that may God the Exalted guide our honoured Queen in a manner that pleases Him. May God the Almighty also guide the progeny of Her Majesty to become established on the Truth and to guiding others towards it. May the attributes of justice and freedom continue to remain the guiding principles of the British Monarchy. I once again congratulate Her Majesty from my heart on this occasion of great joy. I present my heartfelt and sincere congratulations to our noble Queen.

With best wishes and with prayers,

Yours Sincerely,

MIRZA MASROOR AHMAD
Khalifatul Masih V
Head of the worldwide
Ahmadiyya Muslim Community

LETTER TO THE SUPREME
LEADER OF THE ISLAMIC
REPUBLIC OF IRAN

بِسْمِ اللهِ الرَّحْمٰنِ الرَّحِيْمِ

نَحْمَدُهُ وَ نُصَلِّیْ عَلٰی رَسُوْلِهِ الْکَرِیْمِ

وعلٰی عبدِهِ المسیح الموعود

خدا کے فضل اور رحم کے ساتھ

هوالناصــر

MIRZA MASROOR AHMAD
HEAD OF THE AHMADIYYA COMMUNITY
IN ISLAM

16 Gressenhall Road
Southfields, London
SW18 5QL, UK

14 May 2012

Supreme Leader of the Islamic Republic of Iran
Ayatollah Syed Ali Hosseini Khamenei
Tehran, Iran

Respected Ayatollah,

Assalamo Alaikum Wa Rehmatullahe Wa Barakatohu,

Allah the Almighty has enabled you to serve Islam in Iran and presently, the Government of Iran also functions under your auspices. This requires that we strive to our utmost to convey the correct Islamic teachings to the world. As Muslims, we should endeavour to teach the world to live in peace, love and harmony. In particular, Muslim leaders need to urgently pay heed to this. For this reason, it is my request to you to draw the attention of your Government towards its responsibilities to establishing peace in the world. If Iran is attacked it has the right to defend itself to save the country, however it should not instigate aggression and take the first step forward into any conflict. Instead, an effort should be made to leave aside religious differences and to try and unite upon common values. It is this very approach that we find was adopted in the history of Islam.

I am writing this letter to you for the reason that I am a believer, Successor and the Khalifa of the Promised Messiah and Imam Mahdi (peace be upon him), whose advent in this age was prophesied by the Holy Prophet Muhammad (peace be upon him). The Community he established is known as the Ahmadiyya Muslim Community. With the Grace of Allah, the Community has now spread to 200 countries of the world and has millions of devoted followers across the globe. It is our ardent desire to guide the world towards living in mutual love and peace. To this end, I constantly draw the attention of people from all walks of life. Hence, I recently wrote to the Prime Minister of Israel, the President of the United States of America and also other world leaders. I have also written to Pope Benedict XVI in this regard.

As the spiritual leader of a large Islamic nation, I hope that you will come to agree that if the entire Muslim *Ummah* unites and works together, world peace can be established. We should not pointlessly add fuel to enmities and grudges; rather, we should search for opportunities to establish peace and tranquillity. Further, even enmity or opposition against others should not be devoid of justice. This is what we have been taught in the Holy Qur'an:

'O ye who believe! be steadfast in the cause of Allah, bearing witness in equity; and let not a people's enmity incite you to act otherwise than with justice. Be always just, that is

nearer to righteousness. And fear Allah. Surely, Allah is aware of what you do.' (Surah Al-Ma'idah, Verse 9).

May Allah enable the entire Muslim *Ummah* and all Muslim governments to understand my message so that they prepare themselves to play their respective roles in an effort to establish peace in the world.

It is my love for mankind, developed out of a love for the entire Muslim *Ummah*, and also because of being a member of the *Ummah* of the '*Mercy for all mankind*' myself, that has led me to writing this letter. May Allah enable the leaders of the world to understand my words and may they actively play a role in establishing world peace. Otherwise, if the haste and recklessness of any nation leads to a full blown war between two nations, such a conflict will not be limited to only those countries; rather the flames of war will engulf the entire world. Thus, it is entirely plausible that a World War will break out, which will not be fought with conventional weapons, but rather with atomic weapons. A nuclear war will result in such horrific and devastating consequences that its aftermath will not only affect those present in the world at the time, rather the long-term effects of such a war would provide the terrifying 'gift' to future generations of being born with disabilities and defects. For this reason, no country should assume they are safe from the impending destruction.

Therefore, once again, in the name of Allah and His Messenger and out of compassion and love for humanity, I request you to play your role in establishing peace in the world.

With best wishes and with prayers,

Wassalam,
Yours Sincerely,

MIRZA MASROOR AHMAD
Khalifatul Masih V
Head of the worldwide
Ahmadiyya Muslim Community

GLOSSARY

Aḥmadiyya Muslim Jamā**'at**—The Community of Muslims who have accepted the claims of Ḥaḍrat Mirza Ghulam Ahmad[as] of Qadian as the Promised Messiah and Mahdi. The Community was established by Ḥaḍrat Mirza Ghulam Ahmad[as] in 1889, and is now under the leadership of his fifth *khalīfah*—Ḥaḍrat Mirza Masroor Ahmad (may Allah be his help). The Community is also known as **Jam**ā**'at-e-Aḥmadiyya**. A member of the Community is called an **Aḥmadī Muslim** or simply an **Aḥmadī**.

Al-Imam al-Mahdi—The title given to the Promised Reformer by the Holy Prophet Muhammad[sa]; it means the guided leader.

Āmīn—A term said after a prayer meaning, 'May Allah make it so.'

Assalāmu 'alaikum wa raḥmatullāhe wa barakātohū—Traditional Islamic greeting, meaning, may peace be on you, and the mercy of Allah and His grace.

Ḥaḍrat—A term of respect used for a person of established righteousness and piety; lit. 'His/Her Holiness.'

Holy Prophet[sa]—A term used exclusively for the Founder of Islam, Ḥaḍrat Muhammad, may peace and blessings of Allah be upon him.

Holy Quran—The Book sent by Allah for the guidance of mankind. It was revealed word by word to the Holy Prophet Muhammad[sa] over a period of twenty-three years.

Khalīfah—Successor. A Khalīfah of Allah is a term used for a Prophet. Khalīfah of a Prophet refers to his Successor who continues his mission.

Khalīfatul-Masīḥ—A term used by the Aḥmadiyya Muslim Jamāʿat to denote the Successors of the Promised Messiah[as].

Khilāfat—The literal meaning of the term is successorship.

Mahdi—The literal translation of this word is 'the guided one'. This is the title given by the Holy Prophet Muhammad[sa] to the awaited Reformer of the Latter Days.

The Promised Messiah—This term refers to the Founder of the Aḥmadiyya Muslim Jamāʿat, Ḥaḍrat Mirza Ghulam Ahmad[as] of Qadian. He claimed that he had been sent by Allah in accordance with the prophecies of the Holy Prophet[sa] about the coming of *al-Imam al-Mahdi* (the Guided Leader) and Messiah.